YEARBOOK 2013/14

LOTTERY FUNDED

Supported using public funding by
ARTS COUNCIL
ENGLAND

First published in 2013 by the Royal Opera House
in association with Oberon Books Ltd
Oberon Books Ltd
521 Caledonian Road, London N7 9RH
Tel +44 (0)20 7607 3637
info@oberonbooks.com
www.oberonbooks.com

Cover and book design: James Illman

Editor: Andrew Walby

For the Royal Opera House:

Commissioning Editor: John Snelson

Project Manager: Will Richmond

Additional contributors: Gerard Davis, Ruth Garner, Amanda Holloway

A catalogue record for this book is available from the British Library.

ISBN 978-1-78319-002-7

Printed and bound by Replika Press PVT Ltd, India

Royal Opera House
Covent Garden
London WC2E 9DD
Box Office +44 (0)20 7304 4000
www.roh.org.uk

Cover image: Marianela Nuñez and Federico Bonelli
in Christopher Wheeldon's *Aeternum* ©ROH/Johan Persson, 2013

Inside front cover and page 1: The Royal Ballet
in Wayne McGregor's *Raven Girl* ©ROH/Johan Persson, 2013

Page 96 and inside back cover: Genesia Rosato, Alina Cojocaru,
Romany Pajdak, Elizabeth Harrod, Itziar Mendizabal and Beatriz Stix-Brunell
rehearsing Kenneth MacMillan's *Las hermanas* ©ROH/Bill Cooper, 2012

Back cover: Fumi Kaneko and Nehemiah Kish
in Alexei Ratmansky's *24 Preludes* ©ROH/Johan Persson, 2013

Kevin O'Hare portrait on page 4 by Teri Pengilley

Contents

Welcome from Kevin O'Hare

Welcome to our 2013/14 Yearbook.

The 2012/13 Season was a tremendously busy and rewarding one, containing no less than five new works as well as some welcome additions to the repertory, all of which are recorded in these pages.

There were many exciting debuts from our wonderful Principal dancers as well as from more junior members of the Company, and they were all thrilling to watch. The end of the Season saw departures from some of the Company's most familiar faces including Principals Leanne Benjamin and Mara Galeazzi, who both retired after long and wonderful careers with the Company, and Alina Cojocaru and Johan Kobborg who gave many memorable performances with The Royal Ballet and will go on to pursue new artistic challenges.

A succession of successful performances was given in the Linbury Studio Theatre, and we welcome Emma Southworth who joins us this Season as Senior Producer for our Studio Programme. Meanwhile our Education and Cinema programmes continue to go from strength to strength.

The Season ahead is set to be equally stimulating and challenging with not one but two new full-length productions: Carlos Acosta's *Don Quixote* and Christopher Wheeldon's *A Winter's Tale*, based on Shakespeare's play. There are also three new one-act ballets from British choreographers to look forward to – from Wayne McGregor (our Resident Choreographer), David Dawson and Alastair Marriott, and a host of familiar and well-loved classic and contemporary ballets from our repertory.

I do hope you continue to enjoy the tremendous variety of our work, the versatility and theatricality of our fantastic dancers and choreographers, and the many creative artists who will be working with us throughout the coming year. We very much look forward to having you with us.

Kevin O'Hare
Director, The Royal Ballet

The Company
The Royal Ballet 2012/13 Season

The 2012/13 Season marked two significant anniversaries for The Royal Ballet: 25 years since the death of Founder Choreographer Frederick Ashton, and 20 years since the death of Kenneth MacMillan, Principal Choreographer from 1977 to 1992. The work of these two key figures in the Company's heritage, both of whom became Director, was celebrated in two exhilarating mixed programmes: a MacMillan triple in November, and performances featuring five of Ashton's works in February. In addition to well-known classics of the repertory, each programme offered the opportunity to discover a neglected masterpiece: MacMillan's rarely seen *Las hermanas* was staged for the Company by Ray Barra, who created the role of The Man with MacMillan in Stuttgart in 1963, and Ashton's haunting *Monotones* I and II were performed together for the first time at Covent Garden since 1992. The Ashton programme saw the reunion of Tamara Rojo (now Artistic Director of English National Ballet) and Sergei Polunin, who both left the Company last Season, in three performances of *Marguerite and Armand*. This showpiece, originally created on Margot Fonteyn and Rudolf Nureyev, was also danced to much acclaim by Zenaida Yanowsky and Federico Bonelli.

Another anniversary celebrated with performances in the 2012/13 Season was the centenary of the London premiere of Mikhail Fokine's *The Firebird*, which was given its first performance at Covent Garden by Sergey Diaghilev's Ballets Russes. Royal Ballet Music Director Barry

Wordsworth brought Stravinsky's magnificent score vividly to life, conducting the Orchestra of the Royal Opera House. This darkly exotic 20th-century classic was performed in a mixed programme with Jerome Robbins's romantic *In the Night* and Act III of Nureyev's version of Marius Petipa's *Raymonda*, marking yet another anniversary – 20 years since Nureyev's death.

Company classics

The Season also featured several full-length Company classics. Peter Wright's production of *The Nutcracker* triumphed once again, delighting audiences over the Christmas period. This revival saw several significant debuts: First Artist Fumi Kaneko (promoted to Soloist for the 2013/14 Season) made an unscheduled debut as the Sugar Plum Fairy, Artists Francesca Hayward and Tristan Dyer (both promoted to First Artist) danced Clara and Hans-Peter, and First Soloist Ryoichi Hirano made his role debut as the Prince. John Cranko's passionate and tragic ballet *Onegin*, performed the following month, also provided opportunities for many stunning debuts: from Marianela Nuñez, Sarah Lamb and Valeri Hristov in the Principal roles, and also from Dawid Trzensimiech, Valentino Zucchetti, Nehemiah Kish, Meaghan Grace Hinkis and Yasmine Naghdi. The Company also welcomed Jason Reilly from Stuttgart Ballet as a guest, who danced Onegin in four performances with Alina Cojocaru.

The revival of Anthony Dowell's classic production of *Swan Lake*, which opened the Season, was danced on the first night by Marianela Nuñez and Thiago Soares. Russian dancer Natalia Osipova made her debut with the Company opposite Carlos Acosta as Prince Siegfried. In April 2013 Kevin O'Hare announced that Osipova would join the Company as a Principal at the start of the 2013/14 Season.

Another Petipa favourite, *La Bayadère*, returned in April. Its virtuosic solos and ensembles always provide a platform for the technical excellence and artistry of the Company, and this revival brought exciting debut performances from Federico Bonelli, Nehemiah Kish and Steven McRae as the noble warrior Solor, from Yuhui Choe, Claire Calvert and Itziar Mendizabal as the imperious Gamzatti, and from Hikaru Kobayashi as the temple dancer Nikiya.

MacMillan's dark and dramatic masterpiece *Mayerling* was the final full-length ballet of the Season, and saw several memorable role debuts including from Bennet Gartside, who stepped in for an indisposed Johan Kobborg as Crown Prince Rudolf, dancing with Mara Galeazzi as Mary Vetsera.

Contemporary revivals, new work and new additions

From celebrating heritage to nurturing new choreography, the Season also saw contemporary revivals, two additions to the Royal Ballet repertory, and several new commissions.

Artistic Associate Christopher Wheeldon's fantastical ballet *Alice's Adventures in Wonderland* – quickly becoming a favourite of the Royal Ballet

7

repertory – was given its second revival, with Yuhui Choe giving her first sparkling performance in the title role. The ballet was also broadcast live to cinemas with Sarah Lamb and Federico Bonelli in the Principal roles, and was received enthusiastically around the world.

The Royal Opera House's gala celebration of HM The Queen's Diamond Jubilee on 30 October saw the world premieres of three new *pas de deux*: Royal Ballet Resident Choreographer Wayne McGregor's *Ambar*, Alastair Marriott's *In the Hothouse* and Liam Scarlett's *Jubilee pas de deux.*

In November, Scarlett was appointed The Royal Ballet's first Artist in Residence, allowing him to focus exclusively on choreography. He made his final appearance as a dancer with the Company in *Swan Lake* on 24 November. In the same month, his one-act non-narrative ballet *Viscera* (created on Miami City Ballet and first performed in January 2012) was taken into the Royal Ballet repertory, appearing in an electrifying mixed programme with McGregor's *Infra* and, joining the repertory for the first time, Wheeldon's *Fool's Paradise.* Scarlett's *Hansel and Gretel* was not only the choreographer's first full-length narrative ballet for the Company but also The Royal Ballet's first full-length commission for the Linbury Studio Theatre. It received its sell-out premiere in May 2013 and will be revived in the 2013/14 Season. Following its huge success in 2011, Arthur Pita's award-winning dance-theatre adaptation of Kafka's *The Metamorphosis*

was revived in the Linbury with Edward Watson returning in the lead role.

A magnificent triple programme in February/March featured three of the Company's male Principals (Acosta, Bonelli, Pennefather) in the title role in Balanchine's *Apollo*, alongside two new works. *24 Preludes* is the first work created on a British company by Russian-born Alexei Ratmansky, currently Artist in Residence with American Ballet Theatre. Set to Chopin's piano preludes, orchestrated by Jean Françaix, Ratmansky delights in the unique qualities of the Royal Ballet Principals, acutely tailoring his choreography to their individual languages of movement. Wheeldon's *Aeternum* is a powerfully emotional work with stunning designs by Jean-Marc Puissant. The choice of music was *Sinfonia da Requiem* by Benjamin Britten, and in the centenary year of the British composer's birth, Wheeldon dedicated *Aeternum* to him.

McGregor's latest commission, *Raven Girl*, closed the Season alongside Balanchine's exquisite *Symphony in C*. Continuing a passion for innovative collaboration, McGregor worked with bestselling novelist Audrey Niffenegger and Academy Award-winning composer Gabriel Yared to create an evocative new fairytale for the Company.

Beyond Covent Garden

Outside the Royal Opera House, fashion photographer and artist Rick Guest presented an exhibition of his photography of Royal Ballet dancers, *Now is all there is – Bodies in Motion*, at The Hospital Club. Leading stylist Olivia Pomp worked with the dancers and Guest to create a series of astounding photographs in a true synthesis of fashion, photography and dance.

It was a bumper Season for awards and honours. Christopher Wheeldon's *Aeternum* won the Olivier Award for Best New Dance Production and Marianela Nuñez won the Olivier for Outstanding Achievement in Dance for her performances in *Aeternum*, *Viscera* and 'Diana and Actaeon' from *Metamorphosis: Titian 2012*. At the National Dance Awards Nuñez also won the Grishko Award for Best Female Dancer, Arthur Pita won for Best Modern Choreography for *The Metamorphosis* and Royal

Ballet Associate Company Ballet Black won the Grishko Award for Best Independent Company. *Metamorphosis: Titian 2012* was nominated for a South Bank Sky Arts Award. James Hay won the Audience Choice Award at the Erik Bruhn Prize in Canada. Christopher Wheeldon became a Foreign Honorary Member of the American Academy of Arts and Sciences. Zenaida Yanowsky received a National

9

Opposite page:
Leanne Benjamin
as The Woman in
Kenneth MacMillan's
The Judas Tree

©ROH/Johan
Persson, 2010

Dance Award from the Spanish Ministry of Education and Culture. Wayne McGregor, Monica Mason and Liam Scarlett were all nominated for the h.Club 100 list. And at the LUKAS Awards, celebrating Spanish, Latin American and Portuguese culture in the UK, Carlos Acosta won a lifetime achievement award and Fernando Montaño won the Personality of the Year award, presented by Vivienne Westwood.

The 2012/13 Season was also particularly rich in ballet books. Andrej Uspenski's debut photography collection *Dancers* (Oberon Books, April 2013) offers a unique insight into the lives of Royal Ballet dancers, both on and off the stage, in a beautifully finished compilation. Former Royal Ballet Principal Darcey Bussell's retrospective *A Life in Pictures* (Hardie Grant Books, September 2012) celebrates the ballerina's career in pictures from leading dance photographers. *Titian Metamorphosis* (Art/Books, January 2013) charts the production of 2012's audacious collaborative project with an extensive collection of photographs from rehearsals and finished production, work from the three artists, an introduction from Minna Moore Ede and foreword from Monica Mason. And finally, in preparation for its release in October 2013, Carlos Acosta's debut novel *Pig's Foot* (Bloomsbury) was named one of the 'Waterstones Eleven', an annual list of the most promising fiction debuts.

In addition to their summer tour to Monte Carlo and Japan, the Company travelled nationally and internationally throughout the Season. In March,

Dromore-born Melissa Hamilton, along with Yuhui Choe, Ryoichi Hirano and Dawid Trzensimiech, took part in two performances in Derry-Londonderry in a Gala with the Ulster Orchestra as part of celebrations for the city's nomination as City of Culture 2013. They performed extracts from *Swan Lake* and *pas de deux* by Ashton and MacMillan. Brazilians Roberta Marquez and Thiago Soares also travelled to their home country, joined in Rio de Janeiro by Leanne Benjamin, Sarah Lamb, Steven McRae, Marianela Nuñez and Edward Watson for a weekend of gala performances at the Theatro Municipal that featured Royal Opera Jette Parker Young Artists Justina Gringyte, Dušica Bijelić and Pablo Bemsch. In addition, the dancers took part in a two-day symposium in partnership with the Theatro Municipal and the British Council's TRANSFORM Festival. An Initiative of the ROH Education Department and The Royal Ballet's David Pickering, it brought together local dance teachers, schools and dance companies. After the last performances at Covent Garden, Mara Galeazzi, Itziar Mendizabal, Deirdre Chapman, Edward Watson, Alexander Campbell, Johannes Stepanek and Marcelino Sambé travelled to Snape to perform the world premiere of Kim Brandstrup's *Ceremony of Innocence* at the Aldeburgh Festival – a tremendous success.

The end of the Season

The end of the 2012/13 Season brought some departures from the Company. Principals Leanne

Benjamin, Alina Cojocaru, Mara Galeazzi and Johan Kobborg all announced that they would leave The Royal Ballet. Grant Coyle also left the Company having been répétiteur and notator first with Sadler's Wells Royal Ballet and then The Royal Ballet for over three decades and covering a huge variety of both companies' works.

Leanne Benjamin

In April Leanne Benjamin announced that she would be retiring after 21 years with the Company, 19 of those as a Principal. Benjamin's extraordinary career with The Royal Ballet started with a call from Kenneth MacMillan offering her a position as a First Soloist. She had trained at The Royal Ballet School, danced with such companies as English National Ballet and been a Principal with Sadler's Wells Royal Ballet, but at 28 she longed for the challenging repertory that The Royal Ballet offered.

'Before I joined I'd been doing good roles,' says Benjamin, 'but I felt I hadn't fulfilled my potential in terms of drama. When I joined I did a lot of performances of Ashton, MacMillan, Ashley Page and so on. It was very hard work, but very exciting. Kenneth was around, of course. I was given the incredibly in-depth role of Mary Vetsera in *Mayerling*. Sadly Kenneth passed away just before my first performance, but I did have the chance to work with him on that role.'

Her last performance with the Company at Covent Garden was as Mary Vetsera again: 'It was an incredible night,' she says. 'Flowers were thrown from the

audience; my son came on stage, then the Company. I was so touched by all their warmth and support.'

She's always been a refreshingly grounded dancer. One of the things she's most proud of in her long career is consistency. 'I have missed very few performances. I'm good at knowing how to get back from injuries. I would never give up a show unless I was on my deathbed!' She has every reason to be proud of her attendance record, but it's her vibrant, dramatic and often daring interpretations of many different roles that will go down in Royal Ballet history.

One of her early roles with the Company was in MacMillan's *The Judas Tree*, which featured some of the most violent and realistic choreography ever seen at Covent Garden. What was it like to be that abused Woman on stage? 'I loved it,' she says with a wicked grin. 'No, I mean when you're dancing those things you get into the role. It's very raw and explicit, but – well it's always been an interesting journey here.'

Her personal favourites are MacMillan's one-act ballets. '*Song of the Earth*, *Requiem*, *Gloria*... those pieces that you just plunge yourself into, wrapping yourself round a boy, feeling the emotion. And Kenneth's music choices are always sensational.'

Choreographers such as Alastair Marriott, Kim Brandstrup and Wayne McGregor have been attracted to her intensity, her sense of humour and her technical brilliance – and she's always come up with the goods. 'Wayne approached me when I was nine months pregnant and said, "I'd like you to do my new ballet". I thought, "Coming up to 39 there's no way I can change to modern and contort my body like that – look at me!" But I made it, four months after giving birth.'

That work was *Qualia*, created on her and Edward Watson. He became her most frequent partner in her post-pregnancy decade with the Company. It was a joy and a relief for Benjamin, who had been paired with a series of men in her early years with the Company. 'Its like going out for dinner with a different person every night. So when you get with someone and you feel it's right, there's a connection, it's wonderful.'

Benjamin also pays tribute to some of her other partners over the last two decades, including Tetsuya Kumakawa, Zoltan Solymosi, Jonathan Cope ('in those huge roles, like *Requiem* and *Firebird*, he was wonderful in the lifts'), Johan Kobborg and Steven McRae ('such a generous partner'). She's full of praise for her colleagues: 'I've loved my time with The Royal Ballet. I hope I have left a mark on the Company, but I've got so much out of it. People have helped me to learn so much along the way – particularly that you can't be perfect all the time. I believe in hard work, lots of sweat, in practice as well as on stage. You've got to listen, to trust your coach; it's a bit of luck and talent and being given the right opportunities.'

Her final performance with the Company in Japan was a gala in which she danced the *pas de deux* from *Qualia* with Watson and a *pas de deux* from *Mayerling* with Carlos Acosta.

Royal Ballet Director Kevin O'Hare said: 'Leanne has been such a huge part of The Royal Ballet for the last 21 years – it is hard to imagine the Company without her. I am sure the memory of her unique and very special talent will remain with us through the many roles she created during her long career.'

Benjamin is taking time away from ballet to pursue an architectural design course at Chelsea College of Art and Design. 'Full-on studying! I've done up a lot of properties alongside my career and I like the idea of studying and learning but I have no idea where it will lead.' She hopes to have time for a bit of private coaching, and of course she'll be coming to performances at the Royal Opera House, 'But I've told the dancers that I'm going to enjoy being on the other side, with a glass of wine!'

Alina Cojocaru and Johan Kobborg

Shortly after announcing that they would be leaving the Company at the end of the Season to pursue other artistic challenges, on 5 June Alina Cojocaru and Johan Kobborg gave their last performance with The Royal Ballet at Covent Garden, in one of their signature ballets, *Mayerling*.

Sarah Crompton of the *Daily Telegraph* described the impression they made: 'The couple dance together so often that their limbs seem melded into the same instinctive shapes and her confidence in him allows her to take breathtaking risks in the twisting passion of MacMillan's *pas de deux*.'

13

Kobborg and Cojocaru arrived at The Royal Ballet in the same year, 1999, she from the Kiev Ballet and he from Royal Danish Ballet. Cojocaru made an extraordinary start to her career when, at 15, she won the Gold Medal at the Prix de Lausanne, bringing a six-month scholarship to train at The Royal Ballet School, where she was offered a place in the corps de ballet. She chose instead to go back as a principal to Kiev.

Not for long – in 1999 she joined The Royal Ballet and by 2001 she was promoted to Principal after a performance of Giselle, another of her signature roles. That was the year in which she danced Juliet to Kobborg's Romeo – the start of a great partnership that has continued both on stage and off. Kobborg proposed to her on stage after a performance of *Giselle* in 2011.

Cojocaru has been called a 'classical dancer of luminous clarity', but she is also a dramatic actress; she excels as intense emotional heroines such as Giselle, Ondine, Mary Vetsera, Tatiana, but also in such lighter hearted roles as Lise in *La Fille mal gardée* and such universal favourites as The Sugar Plum Fairy in *The Nutcracker*. While dancing with The Royal Ballet she also performed as a guest with leading international companies including American Ballet Theatre and Hamburg Ballet, and organized gala performances with friends and colleagues for Romanian charities.

Kobborg is a consummately elegant *danseur noble* and an accomplished choreographer who not only contributed his own works but staged a masterpiece from his Danish heritage, August Bournonville's *La Sylphide*, for The Royal Ballet. A popular choice in romantic roles such as Romeo, Des Grieux and Albrecht, he also brought a touch of quiet menace to roles such as Rudolf in *Mayerling* and memorably, the Dancing Master in Danish choreographer Flemming Flindt's *The Lesson*. Over the last few years Kobborg has choreographed works for companies around the globe and enjoyed collaborations with different dancers, saying, 'I hope that some of what I give them will have a life beyond the performance we worked on'. Now 41, he says he will continue to dance but will also be able to take on more choreographic commissions. He won't be short of offers.

At their last performances Kevin O'Hare wished them success for the next phase of their careers. 'Alina and Johan have given many memorable performances as members of The Royal Ballet both at the Royal Opera House and around the world,' he said. 'Over the past ten years I have greatly enjoyed watching their unique partnership develop, as I know our audiences have.'

Mara Galeazzi

Mara Galeazzi has been a member of The Royal Ballet for 21 years. In that time she has acquired a devoted international audience, cultivated a series of successful partnerships and worked tirelessly outside the Company on galas, both independent and for her charity, Dancing for the Children.

She is known for the intense emotion and dramatic energy with which she has infused many of the best-loved roles in the repertory, and especially those in the MacMillan canon, over her long career.

In her last *Mayerling* on 13 June, she danced Mary Vetsera to Edward Watson's Crown Prince Rudolf to rapt audiences. The performance was broadcast live to outdoor screens all over the UK, and inside the auditorium there was a feeling of deep appreciation and a sentiment of heartfelt farewell.

'At the end of my last *Mayerling* I was exhausted,' she says, 'but I just wanted to do it again! It was the same with my last *Manon* on tour in Monaco – also with Edward – I had no energy because of the emotion, but it felt like there was enough to get up and do it all over again. It was so enjoyable.'

The first time she danced Mary Vetsera was with Adam Cooper in 1993, not long after she joined while she was still in the corps de ballet. The Company was on tour in Istanbul and, she says, one of the ballerinas was injured, so Monica Mason taught her the role in just ten days:

'Mary Vetsera is so important for me – I know it so well and I enjoy it a lot! I've done it so much that its in my body. But I also love Juliet, Manon, Anastasia, The Woman in *Judas Tree*, The Chosen One in *Rite of Spring*...' and outside the MacMillan repertory she has given many other roles her individual touch: Giselle, Tatiana in Cranko's *Onegin* and the Firebird, to name a few.

15

She has danced these roles with many different partners including Cooper, Robert Tewsley, Irek Mukhamedov, Jonathan Cope, Federico Bonelli, Johan Kobborg, David Makhateli, Thiago Soares and, of course, Watson.

'I did find with Adam, there was something – a connection – in the way we worked together. And when Irek arrived and Adam left, I had a similar relationship with him. It was wonderful to find that connection. And in the last ten years [she was made Principal in 2003] there has been Ed – I've done most with Ed – we started with MacMillan's *My Brother, My Sisters* in 2005. I think from there on we found an understanding just by looking at eachother, and through our body language. We are very different personalities, but I think that has worked really well. It's very organic, and there's a lot of trust.'

As a teenager studying at the school of La Scala in Milan, she was spotted by Michael Messera, who brought her to London for an audition with Anthony Dowell and Monica Mason (who was then Assistant Director of the Company). Galeazzi arrived in London in 1992, speaking not a word of English, and after the audition was invited to join the corps. She was soon dancing Principal roles, recognized for her dramatic flair, and pushed and encouraged by, among others, Ashley Page, Glen Tetley, Irek Mukhamedov and Monica Mason. She has very fond memories of those that have nurtured her talent as a dancer over the years, including Monica Parker, who has staged the revivals of many of the MacMillan works that she has danced, and choreographers Alastair Marriott, who has created a number of pieces on her and Gary Avis, and Wayne McGregor, who created roles on her in *Infra* and *Limen* among other works.

The first choreographer she worked with for The Royal Ballet, during her first month in the Company, was Christopher Wheeldon. At the time Wheeldon was a young choreographer, just out of The Royal Ballet School, and he created some choreography for a workshop at the Riverside Studios in Hammersmith. Mason remembers that MacMillan was with her in the audience for the workshop, which was just three weeks before he died, and, seeing Galeazzi dance Wheeldon's signature lifts and throws in fluid *pas de deux*, he said to Mason: 'I like this girl'.

She danced in Tetley's *La Ronde* in 1993 when it first joined the Royal Ballet repertory, alongside established Principals Darcey Bussell, Viviana Durante, Fiona Chadwick and Leanne Benjamin, and others of his creations that Mara has also danced – *Voluntaries*, *Pierrot Lunaire* – remain among her favourite roles.

'I think I had a special relationship with Glen Tetley but then also with Ashley Page, who pushed me a lot and created many pieces on me' – for example the Olivier Award-winning *Fearful Symmetries* (1995) and *Cheating Lying Stealing*, which Page created to celebrate de Valois's 100th birthday in 1998.

Kevin O'Hare says of her, 'Mara worked her way through the Company's ranks dancing in all The Royal Ballet's repertory but quickly excelled in the dramatic roles making her mark in a series of vivid portrayals of characters such as Juliet, Mary Vetsera and Tatiana in *Onegin*. She has set a great example to the younger members of the Company through her wonderful sense of team work and camaraderie and all her charity work.'

After her last performance in Monaco, she went on to Verona to stage her own gala, 'Mara Galeazzi and Friends', which sold out the stunning Teatro Romano. Then back to London to sell her house and pack up before moving to Oman to live with her husband Jurgen and daughter Maia, who was born in April 2012.

'I think I may still do some dancing' she says. She is working on a handful of projects – and will of course continue working with her charity, Dancing for the Children, with another charity gala planned for 2014. 'But what I'd really love to do is open my own ballet company in Oman! I would also really love to come back and coach some of the MacMillan roles in London, if they would allow me to do that. I would love to pass on all that I have learned over the years from Monica, from Anthony Dowell, from all these people – whatever everyone has passed on to me I'd like to pass the knowledge on.'

Entrances and Exits

Natalia Osipova, Principal Dancer with the Mikhailovsky Theatre, joins the Company as Principal.

Soloist Melissa Hamilton is promoted to First Soloist.

First Artists Olivia Cowley, Elizabeth Harrod and Fumi Kaneko are promoted to Soloist, while Artists Hayley Forskitt, Francesca Hayward and Tristan Dyer are promoted to First Artist.

During the 2012/13 Season Royal Ballet School students Anna Rose O'Sullivan, Luca Acri and Marcelino Sambé all joined the Company as Artists and students Annette Buvoli and David Donnelly join as Artists for the new Season.

Masaya Yamamoto joins the Company as a Prix de Lausanne dancer.

Emma Southworth joins the Company as Senior Producer, The Royal Ballet Studio Programme, for the new Season.

During the Season Liam Scarlett retired from dancing and Jonathan Watkins left the Company.

At the end of the Season Principals Leanne Benjamin, Alina Cojocaru, Mara Galeazzi and Johan Kobborg, and Soloist Brian Maloney left the Company.

Principal Dance Notator and Répétiteur Grant Coyle, and Theresa Beattie, Interim Creative Producer, The Royal Ballet Studio Programme, also left the Company at the end of the 2012/13 Season.

Opposite page:
Mara Galeazzi and Edward Watson at the curtain call after her last performance of *Mayerling* on the main stage

©ROH/Ruairi Watson, 2013

Swan Lake

Choreography
**Marius Petipa and
Lev Ivanov**

*Additional
choreography*
Frederick Ashton
(Act III Neapolitan
dance),
David Bintley
(Act I Waltz)

Music
**Pyotr Il'yich
Tchaikovsky**

Conductors
**Boris Gruzin,
Barry Wordsworth**

Production
Anthony Dowell

Designs
Yolanda Sonnabend

Lighting design
Mark Henderson

Production research
Roland John Wiley

Staging
Christopher Carr

Ballet Master
Gary Avis

Ballet Mistress
Samantha Raine

Principal coaching
**Alexander
Agadzhanov,
Lesley Collier,
Donald MacLeary,
Roland Price,
Christopher
Saunders**

Dance Notators
**Grant Coyle,
Anna Trevien**

Premieres
15 January 1895
(Mariinsky Theatre,
St Petersburg);

13 March 1987
(The Royal Ballet,
this production)

This page:
Tara-Brigitte Bhavnani and Claire Calvert as Two Swans

Opposite page:
Natalia Osipova as Odette and Carlos Acosta as Prince Siegfried

Photographs:
©ROH/Alice Pennefather, 2012

Viscera

Choreography
Liam Scarlett

Music
Lowell Liebermann

Conductor
Barry Wordsworth

Solo piano
Robert Clark

Costume designs
Liam Scarlett

Lighting design
John Hall

*Assistant to the
Choreographer*
Ricardo Cervera

Dance Notator
Amanda Eyles

Premieres
6 January 2012
(Miami City Ballet)

3 November 2012
(The Royal Ballet)

Fool's Paradise

Choreography
Christopher Wheeldon

Music
Joby Talbot

Conductor
Barry Wordsworth

Costume designs
Narciso Rodriguez

Lighting design
Penny Jacobus

Guest Ballet Master
Jason Fowler

*Assistant
Ballet Master*
Jonathan Howells

Premieres
21 September 2007
(Morphoses, Sadler's
Wells Theatre)

3 November 2012
(The Royal Ballet)

This page:
**Members of
The Royal Ballet**
Opposite page:
Brian Maloney
Photographs:
©**ROH/Andrej
Uspenski, 2012**

22

Infra

Choreography
Wayne McGregor

Music
Max Richter

Solo piano
Paul Stobart

Set designs
Julian Opie

Costume designs
Moritz Junge

Lighting design
Lucy Carter

Sound design
Chris Ekers

Ballet Master
Gary Avis

Premiere
13 November 2008
(The Royal Ballet)

This page:

Top:
**Francesca Hayward
and Tristan Dyer**

Bottom:
**Fumi Kaneko and
Dawid Trzensimiech**

Photographs:
©**ROH/Andrej
Uspenski, 2012**

Opposite page:
**Sarah Lamb and
Ryoichi Hirano**

Photograph:
©**ROH/Bill
Cooper, 2012**

24

Concerto

Choreography
Kenneth MacMillan

Music
Dmitry Shostakovich

Conductor
Barry Wordsworth

Solo piano
Kate Shipway

Designs
Jürgen Rose

Lighting design
John B Read

Staging
Christopher Carr

Ballet Master
Gary Avis

Ballet Mistress
Samantha Raine

Principal coaching
Gary Avis,
Christopher Carr,
Lesley Collier

Dance Notator
Grant Coyle

Premieres
30 November 1966
(Berliner Ballett)

17 November 1970
(The Royal Ballet,
this production)

Las hermanas

Choreography
Kenneth MacMillan

Music
Frank Martin

Conductor
Barry Wordsworth

Solo harpsichord
Thomas Trotter

Designs
Nicholas Georgiadis

Lighting design
John B Read

Staging
Ray Barra

Ballet Master
Jonathan Cope

Principal coaching
**Monica Mason,
Ray Barra**

Dance Notator
Grant Coyle

Premieres
13 July 1963
(Stuttgart Ballet)

23 February 1998
(The Royal Ballet,
this production)

This page:
**Melissa Hamilton as
The Youngest Sister
and Thiago Soares
as The Man**

Opposite page:
**Melissa Hamilton as
The Youngest Sister,
Laura Morera as The
Jealous Sister and
Elizabeth McGorian
as The Mother**

Photographs:
©**ROH/Bill
Cooper, 2012**

26

Requiem

Choreography
Kenneth MacMillan

Music
Gabriel Fauré

Conductor
Barry Wordsworth

Soprano
Laura Wright

Baritone
George Humphreys

Royal Opera Chorus

Chorus Master
Renato Balsadonna

Designs
**Yolanda Sonnabend
in association with
Peter Farley**

Lighting design
John B Read

Staging
**Christopher
Saunders**

Ballet Master
**Christopher
Saunders**

Premieres
28 November 1976
(Stuttgart Ballet)

3 March 1983
(The Royal Ballet)

This page:
**Leanne Benjamin
and Carlos Acosta**

Opposite page:
**Roberta Marquez as
the Sugar Plum Fairy
and Steven McRae as
the Prince**

Photographs:
**©ROH/Bill
Cooper, 2012**

28

The Nutcracker

Choreography
**Peter Wright
after Lev Ivanov**

Music
**Pyotr Il'yich
Tchaikovsky**

Original scenario
**Marius Petipa after
E.T.A. Hoffmann's
*Nussknacker und
Mausekönig***

Conductor
Koen Kessels

*Production and
scenario*
Peter Wright

Designs
**Julia
Trevelyan Oman**

Lighting design
Mark Henderson

Production Consultant
Roland John Wiley

Staging
Christopher Carr

Ballet Master
Gary Avis

Ballet Mistress
Samantha Raine

Principal coaching
**Alexander Agadzhanov,
Gary Avis,
Christopher Carr,
Lesley Collier,
Jonathan Cope,
Christopher Saunders**

Dance Notators
**Grant Coyle,
Mayumi Hotta,
Anna Trevien**

Premieres
16 December 1892
(Mariinsky Theatre,
St Petersburg)

20 December 1984
(The Royal Ballet,
this production)

29

The Firebird

Choreography
Mikhail Fokine

Music
Igor Stravinsky

Conductor
Barry Wordsworth

Designs
Natalia Goncharova

Lighting design
John B Read

Original staging
**Sergey Grigoriev and
Lubov Tchernicheva**

Staging
Christopher Carr

Ballet Master
Gary Avis

Ballet Mistress
Samantha Raine

Principal coaching
Jonathan Cope,
Monica Mason

Dance Notator
Grant Coyle

Premieres
25 June 1910
(Sergey Diaghilev's
Ballets Russes)

23 August 1954
(The Royal Ballet,
this production)

This page:
**Mara Galeazzi as
the Firebird and
Edward Watson as
Ivan Tsarevich**

Photograph:
©**ROH/Alice
Pennefather, 2012**

30

Raymonda Act III

Production
Rudolf Nureyev

Choreography
**Rudolf Nureyev after
Marius Petipa**

Music
Aleksandr Glazunov

Conductor
Barry Wordsworth

Designs
Barry Kay

Lighting design
John B Read

Staging
Christopher Carr

Ballet Master
Gary Avis

Ballet Mistress
Samantha Raine

Principal coaching
**Alexander
Agadzhanov,
Lesley Collier,
Jonathan Cope**

Dance Notator
Grant Coyle

Premieres
7 January 1898
(Mariinsky Ballet,
St Petersburg)

27 March 1969
(The Royal Ballet,
this production)

This page:
**Zenaida Yanowsky
as Raymonda and
Nehemiah Kish as
Jean de Brienne
with members of
The Royal Ballet**

Photograph:
**©ROH/Tristram
Kenton, 2012**

31

In the Night

Choreography
Jerome Robbins

Music
Fryderyk Chopin

Solo piano
Robert Clark

Costume designs
Anthony Dowell

Lighting
Jennifer Tipton
recreated by
Les Dickert

Staging
Christine Redpath

Ballet Master
Christopher
Saunders

Premieres
29 January 1970
(New York
City Ballet)

10 October 1973
(The Royal Ballet,
this production)

This page:

Top:
Alina Cojocaru

Bottom:
**Zenaida Yanowsky
and Nehemiah Kish**

Opposite page:
**Sarah Lamb and
Federico Bonelli**

Photographs:
**©ROH/Tristram
Kenton, 2012**

33

Onegin

Choreography
John Cranko

Music
**Kurt-Heinz Stolze
after Pyotr Il'yich
Tchaikovsky**

Conductor
Dominic Grier

Designs
**Jürgen Rose
after original
1969 designs for
Stuttgart Ballet**

Lighting design
Steen Bjarke

Staging
Jane Bourne

Ballet Master
Gary Avis

Ballet Mistress
Samantha Raine

Principal coaching
**Alexander
Agadzhanov,
Jane Bourne,
Lesley Collier,
Jonathan Cope**

**Premieres
13 April 1965
(Stuttgart Ballet)**

**22 November 2001
(The Royal Ballet,
this production)**

This page:
**Marianela Nuñez
as Tatiana and
Thiago Soares
as Onegin**

Photograph:
**©ROH/Bill
Cooper, 2013**

Opposite page:
**Tamara Rojo as
Marguerite and
Sergei Polunin
as Armand**

Photograph:
**©ROH/Tristram
Kenton, 2013**

34

**Marguerite
and Armand**

Choreography
Frederick Ashton

Music
Franz Liszt

Conductor
Emmanuel Plasson

Solo piano
Robert Clark

Orchestration
Dudley Simpson

Designs
Cecil Beaton

Lighting design
John B Read

Staging
Grant Coyle

Principal coaching
**Alexander
Agadzhanov,
Jonathan Cope**

Dance Notator
Grant Coyle

**Premiere
12 March 1963
(The Royal Ballet)**

Monotones I and II

Choreography
Frederick Ashton

Music
Erik Satie

Conductor
Emmanuel Plasson

Orchestration
**Claude Debussy,
Roland-Manuel,
John Lanchbery**

Designs
Frederick Ashton

Lighting design
John B Read

Staging
Lynn Wallis

Ballet Master
Gary Avis

Principal coaching
**Anthony Dowell,
Antoinette Sibley,
Lynn Wallis**

Premieres
Monotones II:
24 March 1965
(The Royal Ballet)

Monotones I and II:
25 April 1966
(The Royal Ballet)

36

This page:

Top:
**Federico Bonelli,
Marianela Nuñez
and Edward Watson**

Bottom:
**Ryoichi Hirano,
Christina Arestis and
Nehemiah Kish**

Opposite page:

Top:
**Emma Maguire,
Dawid Trzensimiech
and Akane Takada**

Bottom:
**Romany Pajdak,
Tristan Dyer and
Yasmine Naghdi**

Photographs:
**©ROH/Tristram
Kenton, 2013**

37

Voices of Spring

Choreography
Frederick Ashton

Music
Johann Strauss II

Conductor
Emmanuel Plasson

Costume designs
Julia Trevelyan Oman

Lighting design
John B Read

Principal coaching
Christopher Saunders

Dance Notator
Grant Coyle

Premieres
31 December 1977
(The Royal Opera)

2 April 1981
(The Royal Ballet)

This page:
Yuhui Choe and Alexander Campbell

Opposite page:
Sarah Lamb and Rupert Pennefather

Photographs:
©ROH/Tristram Kenton, 2013

'Méditation'
from Thaïs

Choreography
Frederick Ashton

Music
Jules Massenet

Conductor
Emmanuel Plasson

Costume designs
Anthony Dowell

Lighting design
John B Read

Principal coaching
Jonathan Cope,
Anthony Dowell,
Antoinette Sibley

Dance Notator
Grant Coyle

Premiere
21 March 1971
(The Royal Ballet)

La Valse

Choreography
Frederick Ashton

Music
Maurice Ravel

Conductor
Emmanuel Plasson

Designs
André Levasseur

Lighting design
John B Read

Staging
Christopher Carr

Ballet Mistress
Samantha Raine

Principal coaching
Christopher Carr

Premieres
31 January 1958
(La Scala Ballet, Milan)

10 March 1959
(The Royal Ballet)

24 Preludes

Choreography
Alexei Ratmansky

Music
Fryderyk Chopin

Orchestration
Jean Françaix

Conductor
Barry Wordsworth

Costume designs
Colleen Atwood

Lighting design
Neil Austin

Ballet Master
Christopher Saunders

Dance Notator
Amanda Eyles

Premiere
22 February 2013
(The Royal Ballet)

This page:
Rupert Pennefather

Opposite page:
Zenaida Yanowsky

Photographs:
©ROH/Johan Persson, 2013

40

Aeternum

Choreography
Christopher Wheeldon

Music
Benjamin Britten

Conductor
Barry Wordsworth

Designs
Jean-Marc Puissant

Lighting design
Adam Silverman

Assistant to the Choreographer
Jacquelin Barrett

Dance Notator
Anna Trevien

Premiere
22 February 2013
(The Royal Ballet)

This page:
James Hay

Opposite page:
Members of The Royal Ballet

Photographs:
©ROH/Johan Persson, 2013

42

43

Apollo

Choreography
George Balanchine

Music
Igor Stravinsky

Conductor
Barry Wordsworth

Lighting design
John B Read

Staging
Patricia Neary

Principal coaching
Jonathan Cope,
Patricia Neary

Premieres
12 June 1928
(Sergey Diaghilev's
Ballets Russes)

15 November 1966
(The Royal Ballet,
this production)

This page:

Top left:
**Federico Bonelli
as Apollo**

Photograph:
©ROH/Andrej
Uspenski, 2013

Top right:
**Carlos Acosta
as Apollo**

Bottom:
**Rupert Pennefather
as Apollo, Olivia
Cowley as Calliope,
Sarah Lamb as
Terpsichore and
Itziar Mendizabal
as Polyhymnia**

Photographs:
©ROH/Johan
Persson, 2013

44

The Metamorphosis

Choreography/ Director
Arthur Pita

Music
Frank Moon

Designs
Simon Daw

Lighting design
Guy Hoare

Premiere
19 September 2011
(ROH2)

This page:
Edward Watson as Gregor Samsa

Photograph:
©**ROH/Tristram Kenton, 2011**

45

Alice's Adventures in Wonderland

Choreography
Christopher Wheeldon

Music
Joby Talbot

Conductor
David Briskin

Designs
Bob Crowley

Scenario
Nicholas Wright

Lighting design
Natasha Katz

Projection design
Jon Driscoll and Gemma Carrington

Original sound design
Andrew Bruce for Autograph

Assistant to the Choreographer
Jacquelin Barrett

Ballet Master
Christopher Saunders

Dance Notator
Anna Trevien

Premiere
28 February 2011
(The Royal Ballet)

This page:
Itziar Mendizabal as the Queen of Hearts and Gary Avis as the King of Hearts

Photograph:
©ROH/Johan Persson, 2013

46

La Bayadère

Choreography
**Natalia Makarova
after Marius Petipa**

Music
Ludwig Minkus

Conductor
Valeriy Ovsyanikov

Orchestration
John Lanchbery

Production
Natalia Makarova

Set designs
Pier Luigi Samaritani

Costume designs
Yolanda Sonnabend

Lighting design
John B Read

Revival staging
Olga Evreinoff

Ballet Master
**Christopher
Saunders**

Ballet Mistress
Samantha Raine

Principal coaching
**Alexander
Agadzhanov,
Lesley Collier,
Jonathan Cope,
Olga Evreinoff**

Premieres
23 January 1877
(Mariinsky Theatre,
St Petersburg)

18 May 1989
(The Royal Ballet,
this production)

This page:
**Roberta Marquez
as Nikiya**

Photograph:
**©ROH/Tristram
Kenton, 2013**

47

Mayerling

Choreography
Kenneth MacMillan

Music
**Franz Liszt
arranged and
orchestrated by
John Lanchbery**

Conductor
Martin Yates

Designs
Nicholas Georgiadis

Scenario
Gillian Freeman

Lighting design
John B Read

Staging
**Grant Coyle,
Monica Mason**

Ballet Master
Christopher Saunders

Ballet Mistress
Samantha Raine

Principal coaching
**Lesley Collier,
Jonathan Cope,
Monica Mason**

Dance Notators
**Karl Burnett,
Grant Coyle**

Premiere
14 February 1978
(The Royal Ballet)

48

This page:
**Mara Galeazzi as
Mary Vetsera and
Bennet Gartside as
Crown Prince Rudolf**

Opposite page:

Top left:
**Itziar Mendizabal
as Countess
Marie Larisch**

Top right:
**Emma Maguire as
Princess Stephanie**

Bottom:
**Members of
The Royal Ballet**

Photographs:
**©ROH/Johan
Persson, 2013**

49

Hansel and Gretel

Choreography
Liam Scarlett

Music
Dan Jones

Designs
Jon Bausor

Lighting design
Paul Keogan

Premiere
8 May 2013
(The Royal Ballet)

This page:

Top:
James Hay as Hansel and Leanne Cope as Gretel

Bottom:
Laura Morera as Step-Mother and Bennet Gartside as Father

Opposite page:
Steven McRae as The Sandman

Photographs:
©ROH/Tristram Kenton, 2013

50

2012/13 Season

Raven Girl

A new fairytale by
Audrey Niffenegger

*Adapted, directed
and choreographed
for the stage by*
Wayne McGregor

Music
Gabriel Yared

Conductor
Koen Kessels

Designs
Vicki Mortimer

Lighting design
Lucy Carter

Film design
Ravi Deepres

*Associate
lighting design*
Simon Bennison

Ballet Master
Gary Avis

Dance Notator
Amanda Eyles

Premiere
24 May 2013
(The Royal Ballet)

This page:
**Sarah Lamb as the
Raven Girl and
Eric Underwood as
the Raven Prince**

Opposite page:

Top:
**Sarah Lamb as
the Raven Girl**

Bottom:
**Melissa Hamilton
as the Raven Girl
and Ryoichi Hirano
as the Raven Prince**

Photographs:
©**ROH/Johan
Persson, 2013**

52

Symphony in C

Choreography
George Balanchine

Music
Georges Bizet

Conductor
Koen Kessels

Designs
Anthony Dowell

Lighting design
John B Read

Staging
Patricia Neary

Ballet Master
**Christopher
Saunders**

Ballet Mistress
Samantha Raine

Premieres
28 July 1947
(Paris Opéra Ballet)

20 November 1991
(The Royal Ballet,
this production)

Members of
The Royal Ballet

Photograph:
©ROH/Johan
Persson, 2013

The corps de ballet
by Gerard Davis

All the world's major ballet companies have a corps de ballet. Some of the greatest choreography has been created for them – *Swan Lake*, for example, wouldn't be half the ballet it is without a corps. And an enormous amount of effort goes into getting so many dancers to work together in harmony. All dancers, from the youngest to the most experienced Principals, have spent some time as members of the corps.

The Royal Ballet has a long and distinguished history of producing a disciplined and intrinsically artistic corps de ballet and places great emphasis on the strength of this elegant body of dancers. For the 2013/14 Season the corps consists of 40 dancers. This number fluctuates only slightly from year to year (depending on promotions and new dancers) and matches most international companies.

Looking after the 24 female members is Samantha Raine who herself spent nine years in the corps before she was promoted to Soloist in 2006. This is Raine's second Season as Ballet Mistress, a role she's still growing into but one about which she has very clear ideas.

'I rehearse the dancers and make sure they know what they're doing,' she explains. 'It's up to me to make them look their best and to ensure that they reach the standard the Company expects. I'm always making notes because I want them to build on their performances, not just stay at one level. The performances of *La Bayadère* last Season, for example, improved from the first show to the last.'

Typically the corps will start rehearsing a ballet about three or four weeks before the stage calls. Then there will be up to five or six runs of the full ballet in the studio and on the stage before the first night, all while working on several other productions at the same time. 'The corps perform an incredible range of repertory,' says Raine. 'New and different choreographers are always coming in so you're constantly swapping styles. You can be in a rehearsal doing [Wayne] McGregor one moment, but minutes later you'll be in the next studio doing Balanchine or MacMillan. In one day you can rehearse up to four different styles.'

She's excited about the prospect of her second Season as Ballet Mistress and the opportunities it will throw up for her dancers. 'I'm looking forward to doing *Giselle*. I've always wanted to get my hands on rehearsing the Wilis in Act II because it's such a wonderful corps number and I always loved dancing it myself. It'll also be fun working with Carlos Acosta on his new *Don Quixote*; his energy in the studio is amazing. The dryads number is the big corps piece, but compared to some other ballets it's actually not too demanding a way to start the Season!'

What does she think is the guiding force behind a successful corps?

'It's a combination of things: teamwork, pride in the job and them knowing they're all incredible. The ballets couldn't go on without the corps and, even though each of them is one of many dancers, they're still as special as the Principals on any given evening. For me it's not just about the legs and arms all being in the same lines, it's about creating an atmosphere and a feeling. When they're working as a team it really comes across to the audience.'

With the inevitable injuries to dancers in the corps, the Company calls on the services of students from The Royal Ballet School. Not only does this ensure the show will go on, it also gives the next generation of dancers invaluable time working with the full corps. Joining the Company for the 2013/14 Season are Annette Buvoli and David Donnelly. They've just finished their final year at the School, and Buvoli has already danced in such ballets as *Swan Lake* and *La Bayadère* while Donnelly has performed in *Onegin* and *The Firebird* among others.

'The first time I was one of the snowflakes in *The Nutcracker*,' says Buvoli, 'I was looking out at the auditorium and I almost forgot what I was doing because it was such a big thing for me. When you're on the Covent Garden stage your stomach's just flipping and it's the most amazing thing. I don't want that feeling to go away but I think I'll get more relaxed as I get used to it being my performance space.'

Donnelly recalls, 'I went on for one of the stage calls for *Alice's Adventures in Wonderland*. When

Opposite Page:
The corps de ballet in *Giselle*

©ROH/Tristram
Kenton, 2011

you're brand new you have to quickly get used to the huge set, partnering and trying to remember the counts – all on top of your own dancing! Much of it is just being able to feel comfortable in the studio and stage environments, so the opportunities we've had this year will hopefully make it a relatively smooth transition into our first Season.'

Their first Season with the Company is an important milestone in their careers and it's something over which they're both very enthusiastic. 'We're doing two of my favourites – *Giselle* and *Romeo and Juliet*,' says Buvoli delightedly. 'I'm also looking forward to working on a lot of different ballets. It's great to learn new things; the corps are constantly learning.'

'I don't know how much we're going to do next year,' admits Donnelly. 'But for the new *Don Quixote*, even if I'm just standing at the back holding something, just to be part of it would be amazing. What I'm most excited about is that we'll have guest teachers giving classes and choreographers working on new pieces – it's such an integrated environment.'

'And to be able to watch all of the performances!', adds Buvoli. 'I think it's going to be really nice learning from everyone in the Company; they know so much. I mean, we're just coming out of School so it feels like the end, but it's really just the beginning!'

'So much of the final year of School is focused on the development of the artistry of dancing,' concludes Donnelly. 'In the Company you have to bring that extra dimension to your dancing to be able to create the performance required. It's not just about being technicians able to do the steps; it's a level way above that.'

The hierarchy of the Royal Ballet corps consists of two tiers: Artist and the senior-ranked First Artist. Some dancers will spend most, if not all of their career in the corps while others will ultimately become Soloists or Principals. Yasmine Naghdi is now in her fourth year with the corps and is already a well-established First Artist.

'The satisfaction you get after a performance is the best thing about being in the corps,' she says. 'By that I mean when you've come off stage and you feel as if everything's gone to plan, everyone's worked together and our lines were exactly right. Some of the Principals say they can feel it when the corps have a good energy on stage so we help create the right atmosphere for the whole show.'

How do the dancers in the corps make sure that everything looks so precise and co-ordinated?

'Lines, timings and arm and leg heights all need to be correct so you have to repeat things over and over in rehearsals to make them perfect. You have to be aware of your surroundings and be able to look sideways and around you without making it too obvious because you have to simultaneously perform to the audience. We have to learn to work together, so it's about being a unified body and not just caring about *you*. In *Giselle*, for example, we have to run on very fast and then stop abruptly, so if

one of us went wrong the result would be a comical domino effect. But it's fantastic when everyone gets it right.'

Does she have a favourite corps role?

'Dancing in *Swan Lake* is an amazing feeling but, for me, it's even more rewarding being the lead shade in Act II of *La Bayadère*. All eyes are on us when we perform our entrance and the music is so beautiful. When we've done all those arabesques and the adage section you can hear the audience's appreciation in their applause.'

Performing Olga in *Onegin* last Season has given Naghdi a real thirst for more solo spots but she's fully aware of the role the corps is playing, not only in her own career, but for the Company as a whole.

'It's where people start and where you learn a huge amount; it's a vital time in the career of any dancer and should never be underestimated. Some people may not think it's as important as a Soloist or Principal, but we hold the ballet together. If you take away the corps you lose a major part of the decorative art on the stage. The corps is the backbone of many ballets and an outstanding corps ultimately reflects well on the Company.'

Erico Montes has been a First Artist since 2010 and he's been working in the corps for nine years.

59

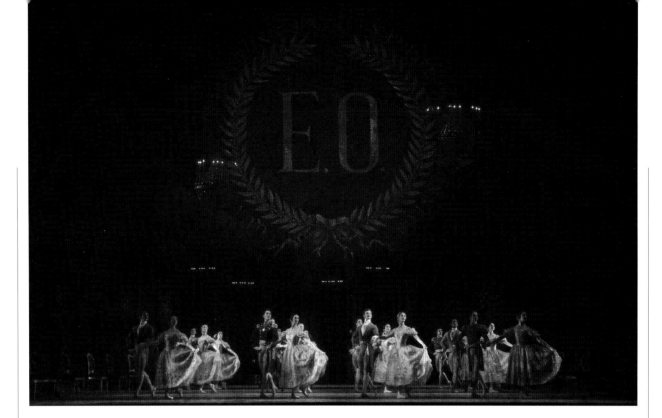

This page:
The corps in
***Onegin*, Act III**

©ROH/Bill
Cooper, 2013

He says that life for the boys is different to that for the girls.

'It's rare that we have a lot of dancing,' he says. 'However, a lot of the Ashton one-act ballets are very hard for the boys, especially *La Valse*, because we do a lot of jumping and lifting. Of the big narrative ballets, *The Sleeping Beauty* is difficult, not because we do a lot of dancing but because we stand on stage in heels for the whole ballet. It's nothing like the shades [*Giselle*] or swans [*Swan Lake*] for the girls, but it is hard to stand for that long and still be engaged with the story.'

Montes is pleased to see *Romeo and Juliet* in the programme for 2013/14. 'It was the first thing I did on the Covent Garden stage as a student. With all of Kenneth MacMillan's ballets you really get involved in the story even if you're in the corps because he creates the feeling of people being natural on stage. In the fight scenes we're not really part of the action

but being so close to it you really do feel like it's all happening to you. It's great fun to do, most people in the Company really enjoy it – especially the girls because they're not in pointe shoes!'

Montes's number one corps role is in *Onegin* because it features 'a bit of everything and plenty of dancing' but another personal favourite is Christopher Wheeldon's *DGV: Danse à grande vitesse*, also being revived for the new Season. 'I've always loved *DGV*; the music is amazing, the steps are great and if you get a good partner it's a lot of fun, particularly during the final section where the music is mainly drums and the stage goes very dark. There's an incredible energy at that point and we're all doing the same thing, including the Principal couples, so you really feel like part of something special.'

It's clear for Montes why he enjoys being in the corps so much: 'The best thing about being in the corps is probably also the worst thing – you're on for every show. It can be very hard, very tiring, but if you really want to be a dancer and if you enjoy the make-up, costumes, lights, live audiences and the thrill of being on stage then you have that several times a week, every week. If you're lucky you also have lots of friends in the corps and you're out there together creating this unique evening for people. I think being part of the corps is just as special as being the star of the show because often the corps *is* the star of the show.'

Before being promoted, Principal Laura Morera spent four years in the corps and has fond memories of the camaraderie generated during her years there, while fully understanding the difficulties involved. 'When you first join the Company it's exciting but, just as with technique, you have to learn how to become a good corps member,' she says. 'You want to be noticed and you need to bring whatever it is that makes you special, but you also need to contain it within the same movement as everyone else – that takes a while to get used to, and I think that's what everyone finds quite hard.'

Other things also proved tricky in the corps, even for a future Principal.

'I loved doing *Giselle* but I found it really hard, line-wise,' she admits. 'I just couldn't visualize it and kept finding myself out of line. It took me a while to get it right, but when I did it was very rewarding and meant I could start enjoying it more.'

Morera is full of admiration for today's corps and appreciates all the hard work they put in. 'When you become a Principal, to the Company you become a lot more detached, partly because sometimes your rehearsals don't coincide with anyone else's for ages. However, if someone asked me to do *Manon* here or with another Company I would always choose The Royal Ballet because the corps not only add to the Principal performances but also create an atmosphere of their own. And if they weren't doing that the shows wouldn't be as good. I feel really proud I did that for other people at one point and that now others are supporting me when I'm performing.'

Morera stresses the importance of the corps in any company: 'Dancing in the corps de ballet teaches you that the show is bigger than you, no matter who you are, and I think it's really important that the corps is treated with the respect they deserve. Sometimes there's a feeling that people are just in the corps as a stepping stone but it's up to everyone to really value the corps and make it clear that they're the heart of the Company.'

So, next time you're watching *Swan Lake*, *Romeo and Juliet* or any ballet in which the corps graces the stage, try and tear your eyes away from centre-stage for a moment. There you'll see dozens of young men and women, some of the finest classical dancers in the world, trying their very best to make the show as magical for you as possible. And then imagine what it would look like without them.

61

Rehearsing the repertory

by Ruth Garner

As the auditorium lights dim, the first notes sound from the orchestra and the dancers take to the stage, it's the culmination of many hours of rehearsal led by The Royal Ballet's expert team of teaching staff – répétiteurs, ballet masters and mistresses, and dance notators.

Many of the current teaching staff and guest teachers either trained or danced under significant figures in the Company's heritage. Royal Ballet Founder Ninette de Valois nurtured a distinctive style for the Company; she engaged the talents of Founder Choreographer Frederick Ashton and Principal Choreographer Kenneth MacMillan, both of whom were to become Director in later years.

The Company has become increasingly international in recent decades, with dancers from over twenty countries across six continents. So, it is vitally important that teachers have an ingrained understanding of The Royal Ballet heritage. Assistant Ballet Master Jonathan Howells explains:

'Monica [Mason, Director of The Royal Ballet, 2002–12] gave me the job because she thought I had that very linear connection – The Royal Ballet style and eye. She really needed people to be able to take that forward. I was taught by Ninette de Valois and I'm probably one of the last people to have had that experience. I've been through the whole system from White Lodge [The Royal Ballet Lower School] through to dancing with the Company. So naturally, I know the Ashton or MacMillan style. One of the worrying things is that that line is disappearing – the generation that created those ballets is now retiring and some have died. It really is that passing on of knowledge to the next generation.'

The Company frequently brings in guest teachers who have expertise with a particular choreographer or work. Last Season, Lynn Wallis (Artistic Director of the Royal Academy of Dance) staged a revival of Ashton's *Monotones* I and II. Following training at The Royal Ballet School and a dancing career with The Royal Ballet Touring Company, Wallis became Ballet Mistress at The Royal Ballet Upper School (1969–82) and during this time was responsible for producing the School's annual performances at the Royal Opera House.

'I had the benefit of working with Ashton and MacMillan when their ballets were part of the Schools' programme', she says. 'I'm very passionate about wanting to pass on all the detail I was given so that in years to come it won't be lost.'

Today's technology allows teachers unprecedented access to recordings of past performances and rehearsals, all slightly different. Wallis stresses that you have to be very selective about the material you work with so that the original choreography isn't diluted over time. Each time she restages *Monotones*, for example, she looks back over all the material she has on the work – her original notes, recordings of the original casts, the Benesh notation score (known to those at The Royal Ballet as 'the Bible') and recordings of subsequent performances.

62

'It is a great way to start', she says. 'I go back over everything, no matter how many times I've staged the work, as you need to be sure that you always stay true to the original.'

The Frederick Ashton Foundation – which exists 'to perpetuate the legacy and work of Frederick Ashton' – is in the process of establishing a programme 'to train (through shadowing schemes) and mentor the Ashton répétiteurs of the future'. Individuals observe and learn from current Ashton répétiteurs in the same way that those répétiteurs observed and learned from Ashton himself. Ricardo Cervera, a First Soloist with the Company, is one such individual and observed Wallis working on the recent revival of *Monotones*.

'We need some new blood – younger people interested in carrying out the work', he says. 'I've been with the Company for 20 years. When I joined, the people who were Ashtonians were still dancing in the Company so I have had that first-hand visual of what the style should look like. I've also danced all the Ashton rep while I've been in the Company. What's interesting about Lynn is that she knows the pieces so well. She actually watched the original

63

process, she knew the original people in it, so she has in her head a version that is true to what Ashton wanted.'

However, teaching The Royal Ballet repertory is not just about preservation of the steps, as Répétiteur Jonathan Cope stresses. Ballet is a living art form and its legacy is as dependent upon what an artist can bring to a role.

'Rather than trying to control the dancers within what we believe is right and within a framework, we've got to allow them to give a show', he explains. 'It's about preserving the ideals. We're a very honest company and we perform very naturally. The world is changing – bodies have changed, dancers have changed, personalities have changed. It's about hanging on to what we believe in. As long as we keep those ideals going then we can evolve.'

'Everybody can bring something different to whatever they are doing', says Ballet Master Gary Avis. 'As long as everyone is doing the right

choreography at the right time, the motivation and interpretation on top of it can be very different.'

There is, however, a fine line between giving the dancers the freedom to make a personal interpretation and being sensitive to the original intent of the choreographer.

'With MacMillan, for example, there's so much emotion', says Ballet Master Christopher Saunders. 'You have to allow all those Rudolfs to look a little different. You can't say, "no, it has to be this, you've got to feel it like that". But when you give them the freedom, they often – without realizing – want to change the steps. It's always good that they should know what it came from.'

Adds Wallis, 'It's a delicate balance and as a producer you have to make informed decisions'.

Musicality is paramount in helping the artists to make their own interpretation of a role and something the teachers strive to bring out in dancers.

'Some dancers have a greater ability to feel the expression and portray the emotion of the music', says Cope. 'Others have more of a tempo-based musicality. It's lovely to have both, really. You can teach an understanding of tempo and rhythm, but to learn the perfume of the music and how it makes you feel is down to the individual artist.'

All the teaching staff of The Royal Ballet enjoyed glittering performance careers before becoming teachers – some still perform with the Company –

Rehearsing the repertory

and they are often teaching roles that they have performed themselves.

'I would say that helps a lot', says Avis, 'because you know the back story of the role, you know the intention, you know the purpose. It's something that's far more than just steps, counts, arms and legs – especially since a lot of our rep is narrative. If you're telling a story, it's all well and good learning what your body is doing, but there's also a reason why. You sometimes have the freedom to add a bit of yourself to the role. Incorporating the character is a big step up from learning the choreography; it's the icing on the cake. That's the thing I really love about nurturing in this role – you can pass on your experiences.'

However, Cope stresses the importance of not putting too much of your own interpretation of a role across to a dancer: 'It's difficult because you don't want them to do it just like you did. A lot of dancers are very good mimics and if you get up and demonstrate, they can actually do a perfect copy of the way you did it and that's not what you want – it's a clone. They've got to be individual.'

With new works, the artistic staff assist the choreographer in the creative process, gaining a detailed understanding of the choreography so that they can confidently teach new casts when the work is revived. Often choreographers allow a considerable amount of interpretative freedom to different casts. Last Season, Cervera assisted Liam Scarlett (The Royal Ballet's Artist in Residence)

in the creation of *Hansel and Gretel*: 'I saw Liam allowing each cast to find their own way of doing the piece. He lets the dancer be artistic and gives them freedom to make the role their own.'

Avis is Ballet Master for works by Wayne McGregor (The Royal Ballet's Resident Choreographer), and was involved in the creation of *Raven Girl*, McGregor's most recent work, at the end of last Season. He witnessed the freedom McGregor allows for the dancers to create roles in collaboration with the choreographer.

'Wayne never likes people to feel that they have to make a carbon copy of the dancer a role has been made on', Avis explains. 'He always says that people

This page:
Jonathan Cope rehearsing Nehemiah Kish for *The Prince of the Pagodas*

©ROH/Johan Persson, 2012

Opposite page:
Alastair Marriott and Jonathan Howells rehearsing 'Trespass' for *Metamorphosis: Titian 2012*

©ROH/Johan Persson, 2012

have to visualize it and be able to make it their own.' McGregor created the lead role on Principal Sarah Lamb. 'There's a lot of Sarah's determination and physicality in the role of the *Raven Girl* herself, but when we are looking at Melissa [Hamilton], she may approach it from another angle with a different thought process.'

The répétiteur or ballet master has to develop an instinctive understanding of the choreographer's style in order to allow new casts interpretative freedom – within boundaries.

'With a non-narrative ballet you teach the steps and the style', explains Howells. 'With a narrative, you do that initially, but then you have to explain what's going on in the story so the dancers really get a sense of it, and that can take quite a long time.' Howells also assists choreographer Alastair Marriott: 'I understand the style he wants and also the way he works. So if I'm left in the studio to rehearse without him, I know exactly what his intentions are.'

'There will always be boundaries', adds Cervera. 'I've worked as a dancer with Liam. I know his style and work. I know what he likes and doesn't like so I would feel confident to say to another dancer, "actually, that's not right – that may feel right to you, but it's not Liam's style".'

Another essential skill is the ability to tailor teaching techniques to individual dancers and temperaments. Here, experience as a performer and appreciation of the pressures that the dancers are under is a great asset.

'You can't just go "blanket version" – "this is how I'm going to teach"', says Lynn Wallis. 'You really need to get into understanding the dancers individually. That's where the respect comes in.'

A strong working relationship between dancer and teacher is imperative. In many respects the Company is very much a 'family', as Cope explains:

'You become like a parent in some respects. You love them all and you can pretty much say anything you want to any of them without offending them. They know that you have their best interests at heart. The disadvantage is that we get used to their weaknesses so when a "clean" eye comes in it's definitely an advantage. They don't let personality sway their opinion, whereas we can't help ourselves but take that into consideration.'

'It can also be hard', adds Saunders, 'because sometimes when you have to say "no", or reprimand someone and they're a good friend, it's not the easiest thing. But that's my job and I have to do it.'

'It's an emotional environment', says Cope. 'They're all artists and they're very expressive emotionally. For the majority of the time there's a lot of pressure on them with the amount of rep that they do, nerves and anxieties. In the studio there is a lot of personality analysis and seeing how it plays out.'

'As a dancer, you literally barely have time to change your shoes,' says Avis. 'You're in one rehearsal room and then straight into another. It's pretty gruelling. There's so much rep and it's so intense. Every day is different with different problems to

contend with, but you should try not to bring these into the studio. Work is work, and the ethic has to be instinctive.'

For all of the teachers, the work is hugely demanding. With schedules often as busy and exhausting as the dancers', many are frequently juggling their workload with commitments outside The Royal Ballet and sometimes their own dancing in rehearsal or on the stage. But all feel that the result of the time and effort invested is immensely rewarding.

'When you're sitting out front watching a performance and you see all of these dancers putting their hearts into it in a way that you've asked them to', says Saunders, 'you just think "they're drawing blood to do it out there, to give a performance". You can't ask for more than that.'

67

Season Preview 2013/14

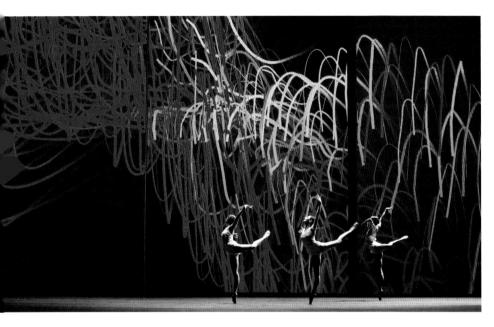

This page:
Eno Henze's designs for David Dawson's *timelapse/ (Mnemosyne)*, Dutch National Ballet, 2011

Photographed by Angela Sterling

Opposite page:
Two of Tim Hatley's costume designs for *Don Quixote*

There is much to enjoy in the new Royal Ballet Season, with several eagerly anticipated new works both on the main stage and in the Linbury Studio Theatre, and the return of many much-loved favourites too.

Royal Ballet Artistic Associate Christopher Wheeldon and the team behind 2011's *Alice's Adventures in Wonderland* are adapting Shakespeare's *The Winter's Tale* into a full-length narrative ballet on the main stage in April/May 2014, with a new score by Joby Talbot. The story provides powerful material for ballet, allowing the portrayal of intense emotions between and within the characters, and the opportunity for the Company to create not just new central roles but a whole vivid world around them.

In September, Principal Guest Artist Carlos Acosta directs himself and The Royal Ballet in his first work for the Company: a sun-drenched production of *Don Quixote*. In choosing to rework Petipa's classic, Acosta follows in a tradition of several great dancer/choreographers who have created dance versions of Cervantes's novel, including Nureyev and Baryshnikov.

There are three further new commissions for the main stage this Season. The first is from David Dawson, also his first for The Royal Ballet. Dawson, who is admired as a visionary choreographer in Europe, is working with designers Eno Henze and Yumiko Takeshima and choreographing to a new score by composer Greg Haines, to be performed live. From the Company, celebrated Royal Ballet dancer/choreographer Alastair Marriott is collaborating with acclaimed designer Es Devlin to make his fifth main-stage work on the Company. And there is a new direction for Resident Choreographer Wayne McGregor, who is working with a phenomenal piece of music by J.S. Bach – *The Art of Fugue* – and designs by American contemporary artist Tauba Auerbach, whose work most recently featured in MoMA's exhibition *Abstract Generation: Now in Print*.

McGregor's new ballet appears in a mixed programme in February, flanked by revivals of one-act ballets from two of the Company's former Resident Choreographers: Ashton's *Rhapsody*, a showpiece for the male dancer originally

68

Don Q.

MERCEDES.

black/purple lace.

Purple embossed velvet

hot pink under.

2013/14 Season

SEPTEMBER/OCTOBER/NOVEMBER

Don Quixote
Ballet in three acts

Choreography
Carlos Acosta
after Marius Petipa

Production **Carlos Acosta**

Music **Ludwig Minkus**
arranged by Martin Yates

Designs **Tim Hatley**

Lighting design
Hugh Vanstone

OCTOBER/NOVEMBER

Romeo and Juliet
Ballet in three acts

Choreography
Kenneth MacMillan

Music **Sergey Prokofiev**

Designs
Nicholas Georgiadis

Lighting design
John B Read

Wednesday 16 October

Don Quixote
Live in cinemas

NOVEMBER

Chroma
Ballet in one act

Choreography
Wayne McGregor

Music **Joby Talbot and
Jack White III** arranged by
Joby Talbot orchestrated
by Christopher Austin

Set designs **John Pawson**

Costume designs
Moritz Junge

Lighting design
Lucy Carter

New David Dawson
Ballet in one act

Choreography
David Dawson

Music **Greg Haines**

Set designs **Eno Henze**

Costume designs
Yumiko Takeshima

Lighting design
Bert Dalhuysen

The Rite of Spring
Ballet in one act

Choreography
Kenneth MacMillan

Music **Igor Stravinsky**

Designs **Sidney Nolan**

Lighting design
John B Read

DECEMBER/JANUARY

The Nutcracker
Ballet in two acts

Choreography
Peter Wright
after Lev Ivanov

Music
Pyotr Il'yich Tchaikovsky

Original scenario
Marius Petipa after E.T.A.
Hoffman's *Nussknacker
und Mausekönig*

Production and scenario
Peter Wright

Designs
Julia Trevelyan Oman

Lighting design
Mark Henderson

Production Consultant
Roland John Wiley

DECEMBER/JANUARY

Jewels
Ballet in three acts

Choreography
George Balanchine

Music **Gabriel Fauré**
('Emeralds')
Igor Stravinsky
('Rubies')
Pyotr Il'yich Tchaikovsky
('Diamonds')

Set designs
Jean-Marc Puissant

Costume designs
Barbara Karinska

Lighting
Jennifer Tipton

Thursday 12 December

The Nutcracker
Live in cinemas

JANUARY

Hansel and Gretel
Ballet in two acts

Choreography
Liam Scarlett

Music
Dan Jones

Designs
Jon Bausor

Lighting design
Paul Keogan

JANUARY/FEBRUARY

Giselle
Ballet in two acts

Choreography
Marius Petipa after Jean
Coralli and Jules Perrot

Music
Adolphe Adam revised
by John Horovitz

Scenario
Théophile Gautier
after Heinrich Heine

*Production and
additional choreography*
Peter Wright

Designs
John Macfarlane

Original lighting
Jennifer Tipton

Monday 27 January

Giselle
Live in cinemas

FEBRUARY

Rhapsody
Ballet in one act

Choreography
Frederick Ashton

Music
Sergey Rachmaninoff

Designs
Jessica Curtis

Lighting design
Neil Austin

▶

choreographed for Mikhail Baryshnikov and recently performed to terrific acclaim by Steven McRae, and MacMillan's haunting *Gloria*, always poignantly captured by the Company's dancers.

Alongside the new Dawson work in November are revivals of McGregor's now classic *Chroma* and MacMillan's mesmerizing *The Rite of Spring*, celebrating the centenary of Stravinsky's blistering score.

Following the well-received revival of Jerome Robbins's *In the Night* during the 2012/13 Season, his rarely seen comic masterpiece *The Concert* makes a welcome return to the repertory in May/June, with the new Marriott as well as Ashton's magical adaptation of Shakespeare, *The Dream*.

Royal Ballet Artist in Residence Liam Scarlett's one-act narrative for the main stage *Sweet Violets*,

which was first performed in 2012, will appear in a thrilling mixed programme with Balanchine's ethereal *Serenade* and Wheeldon's high-energy *DGV: Danse à grande vitesse*, to Michael Nyman's compelling score.

Audiences will be spoilt for choice with welcome revivals of some of the most popular and enduring classics of the Royal Ballet repertory: MacMillan's *Romeo and Juliet*, Peter Wright's timeless productions of *The Nutcracker* and *Giselle*, Balanchine's *Jewels* and Monica Mason and Christopher Newton's production of the De Valois/Sergeyev *The Sleeping Beauty*. All will present great opportunities to see the stars of The Royal Ballet excelling in many of their most famous roles.

The Royal Ballet Studio Programme is at a stage of exciting development, creating a new programme of work that joins the dance programme in the Linbury Studio Theatre and other choreographic projects with the main stage programme, working with both young and established choreographers, from inside the Company and from the wider dance community.

The annual staging of *Draft Works*, which provides a platform for experimental choreography created by Royal Ballet dancers, will be presented in June. The Studio Programme has also commissioned work by Choreographic Affiliates Mayuri Boonham and Alexander Whitley alongside Ben Wright's bgroup and HeadSpaceDance.

70

The Linbury will play host to a wealth of visiting talent, from companies including National Dance Company Wales, De Oscuro, Company Chameleon, Phoenix Dance Theatre, the London International Mime Festival and Ballet Black. In July 2014 New York City Ballet Principal Dancer Wendy Whelan brings an evening of contemporary work to the Linbury.

The Studio Programme brings back Liam Scarlett's *Hansel and Gretel*, and in the autumn Scarlett will also choreograph a specially commissioned *pas de deux* for Zenaida Yanowsky and Rupert Pennefather as part of Fall for Dance at City Centre in New York. Arthur Pita's *The Metamorphosis*, first produced in the Linbury, will also be performed in New York, staged at the Joyce Theatre at the end of September, with Edward Watson as Gregor Samsa.

In an exciting exchange programme that saw Steven McRae take on the role of Lankendem in *Le Corsaire* with American Ballet Theatre in June 2013, ABT Principal Cory Stearns will perform with The Royal Ballet at Covent Garden in December, partnering Lauren Cuthbertson in *The Nutcracker*.

At the end of the Season, the annual Company tour will include The Royal Ballet performing at the newly restored Bolshoi Theatre in Moscow.

Don Quixote, *The Nutcracker*, *Giselle*, *The Sleeping Beauty* and *The Winter's Tale* will all be broadcast live in cinemas as part of the Royal Opera House Live Cinema Season, opening up the Company's work to audiences all over the world.

New Wayne McGregor
Ballet in one act
Choreography
Wayne McGregor
Music **J.S. Bach**
Designs
Tauba Auerbach
Lighting design
Lucy Carter

Gloria
Ballet in one act
Choreography
Kenneth MacMillan
Music
Francis Poulenc
Designs
Andy Klunder
Lighting design
John B Read

FEBRUARY/MARCH

The Sleeping Beauty
Ballet in a prologue and three acts
Choreography
Marius Petipa, with additional choreography by Frederick Ashton, Anthony Dowell and Christopher Wheeldon
Music
Pyotr Il'yich Tchaikovsky
Production **Monica Mason and Christopher Newton after Ninette de Valois and Nicholas Sergeyev**
Designs **Oliver Messel**
Additional designs **Peter Farmer**
Lighting design **Mark Jonathan**

Wednesday 19 March

The Sleeping Beauty
Live in cinemas

APRIL/MAY

The Winter's Tale
Ballet in four acts
Choreography
Christopher Wheeldon
Music **Joby Talbot**
Designs **Bob Crowley**
Lighting design
Natasha Katz

APRIL

New Mayuri Boonham
Ballet in one act
Choreography
Mayuri Boonham

Monday 28 April

The Winter's Tale
Live in cinemas

MAY

The Measures Taken
Ballet in one act
Choreography
Alexander Whitley
Music **Rutger Zuydervelt**
Software Artists
Marshmallow Laser Feast
Lighting design
Lee Curran

MAY

Serenade
Ballet in one act
Choreography
George Balanchine
Music
Pyotr Il'yich Tchaikovsky
Costume designs
Barbara Karinska
Lighting design
John B Read

Sweet Violets
Ballet in one act
Choreography
Liam Scarlett
Music
Sergey Rachmaninoff
Designs
John Macfarlane
Lighting design
David Finn

DGV: Danse à grande vitesse
Ballet in one act
Choreography
Christopher Wheeldon
Music
Michael Nyman
Design
Jean-Marc Puissant
Lighting
Jennifer Tipton

JUNE

The Dream
Ballet in one act
Choreography
Frederick Ashton
Music
Felix Mendelssohn
Designs
David Walker
Lighting design
John B Read

New Alastair Marriott
Ballet in one act
Choreography
Alastair Marriott
Set designs
Es Devlin
Lighting design
Bruno Poet

The Concert
Ballet in one act
Choreography
Jerome Robbins
Music
Fryderyk Chopin, orchestrated by Clare Grundeman
Set designs
Saul Steinberg
Costume designs
Irene Sharaff
Lighting
Jennifer Tipton

JUNE

Draft Works

A Company Chronology

1931 20 January Bizet's opera *Carmen* is staged at the newly reopened Sadler's Wells Theatre. The dancers in it come from a fledgling ballet company, the Vic-Wells Opera Ballet, under the creative direction of their founder Ninette de Valois. The result of many developments of this Company – always under De Valois' leadership – would eventually be The Royal Ballet.

5 May The Company gives its own performance of short works by De Valois at Lilian Baylis's Old Vic theatre. It is Baylis's use of dancers in her operas and plays that gives De Valois the chance to bring her Company together. **July** The Camargo Society presents the Company in a programme that includes De Valois' *Job* and two works by Frederick Ashton, a young dancer also beginning to make his mark as a choreographer.

1932 January Alicia Markova becomes a regular Guest Artist alongside Anton Dolin. **March** *Les Sylphides* is revived with Markova and Dolin. **September** The Company tours for the first time together, to Denmark. **October** Act II of *Le Lac des cygnes* marks the Company's first foray into the classical repertory.

1933 March Nicholas Sergeyev presents the full-length *Coppélia* with Lydia Lopokova as Swanilda. He had been the *régisseur general* of the Mariinsky Theatre, but fled Russia after the October Revolution, bringing the written notation necessary to stage many classic Russian ballets.

1934 January Sergeyev puts on *Giselle* with Markova and Dolin. **April** *Casse-Noisette* is presented, again by Sergeyev. **20 November** The full *Le Lac des cygnes* is presented with Markova and Robert Helpmann, who had recently been promoted to Principal with the Company.

1935 Ashton is signed up as a performer and Resident Choreographer. **20 May** De Valois' *The Rake's Progress* has its first performance, with Markova as the Betrayed Girl. **26 November** Ashton's *Le Baiser de la fée* receives its premiere, with the young Margot Fonteyn in the cast.

1937 The Company represents British culture at the International Exhibition in Paris. **16 February** The premiere of Ashton's *Les Patineurs*. **27 April** A further Ashton premiere

with *A Wedding Bouquet*. **5 October** De Valois' *Checkmate* receives its first performance in London. **25 November** Lilian Baylis dies.

1939 2 February Sergeyev puts on *The Sleeping Princess* with Fonteyn and Helpmann in the lead roles. **1 September** Germany invades Poland; in response, Britain, France, Australia and New Zealand declare war on Germany.

1940 23 January The first performance of Ashton's *Dante Sonata*. **May** The Company travels to the Netherlands for a small tour, but the advancing German army forces a hurried escape. **November** The Company begins to tour throughout Britain during wartime.

1941 The New Theatre, St Martin's Lane, becomes the Company's home for much of the war, and *The Sleeping Princess* is again staged.

1942 19 May The first performance of Helpmann's ballet *Hamlet*, with Helpmann in the title role.

1944 26 October Helpmann's *Miracle in the Gorbals* receives its premiere.

1945 The Company undertakes a tour of the Continent with the Entertainments National Service Association (ENSA), a forces organization. **May 8th** The war ends in Europe.

1946 20 February The Company becomes resident at Covent Garden, and reopens the Royal Opera House with *The Sleeping Beauty*. **24 April** Ashton's *Symphonic Variations* is performed for the first time.

1947 February De Valois invites Léonide Massine, one of the biggest stars of Diaghilev's Ballets Russes, to revive *The Three-Cornered Hat* and *La Boutique fantasque*.

1948 23 December Ashton's *Cinderella* receives its premiere: it is the Company's first home-grown full-length ballet.

1949 9 October The Company presents *The Sleeping Beauty* in New York, the start of a hugely successful tour that takes in many cities in the USA and Canada.

Opposite page:

Top:
Margot Fonteyn as Lady Dulcinea and Robert Helpmann as Don Quixote in the Sadler's Wells Ballet production of *Don Quixote* (1950)

©Carl Perutz-Magnum

Bottom:
Nadia Nerina as The Faded Beauty and Leslie Edwards as The Hypnotist in the Sadler's Wells Ballet production of *Noctambules* (1956)

©Michael Dunne, Studio five

1950 20 February The first performance of De Valois' *Don Quixote*. **5 April** George Balanchine and his New York City Ballet make their first European visit, Balanchine reviving his *Ballet Imperial* for Sadler's Wells Ballet. **5 May** Roland Petit's creation for the Company, *Ballabile*, receives its premiere. **September** The Company embarks on a five-month, 32-city tour of the USA.

1951 21 August Music Director Constant Lambert, one of the chief architects of the Company with De Valois and Ashton, dies aged 45.

1952 3 September The first performance of Ashton's *Sylvia*.

1953 2 June Coronation gala for HM The Queen, which includes a specially devised ballet by Ashton for the occasion, *Homage to the Queen*.

1954 23 August For the 25th anniversary of Diaghilev's death, the Company joins the Edinburgh Festival tributes with a performance of *The Firebird*; Fonteyn dances the title role.

1956 1 March Kenneth MacMillan creates his first ballet for the Sadler's Wells Ballet, *Noctambules*. **31 October** The Sadler's Wells Ballet, the Sadler's Wells Theatre Ballet and the School are granted a Royal Charter – the main Company becoming The Royal Ballet.

1957 1 January John Cranko's *The Prince of the Pagodas*, to a new score by Benjamin Britten, is given its first performance at Covent Garden. It is the first full-length work to a modern commissioned score to be presented in the West.

1958 27 October Ashton's new ballet *Ondine*, created for Fonteyn, opens with her in the title role; the new score is by Hans Werner Henze.

1959 13 March MacMillan's *Danses concertantes*, created for Sadler's Wells Theatre Ballet in 1955, opens at Covent Garden.

1960 28 January The premiere of Ashton's 'tribute to nature', *La Fille mal gardée* with Nadia Nerina dancing the role of Lise to David Blair's Colas.

1961 15 June The Company makes its first tour of Russia presenting *Ondine* on the first night; an exchange agreement sees the Kirov Ballet perform at Covent Garden.

73

1962 21 February Rudolf Nureyev, having controversially defected from the Kirov in 1961, makes his debut as Albrecht to Fonteyn's Giselle. **3 May** MacMillan's new version of *The Rite of Spring*, with Monica Mason as The Chosen Maiden, is given its first performance.

1963 12 March Ashton's *Marguerite and Armand*, created for Fonteyn and Nureyev, opens. **7 May** De Valois retires as Director of the Company and Ashton succeeds her, while De Valois becomes supervisor of The Royal Ballet School. **28 November** Nureyev's first staging for The Royal Ballet is the 'Kingdom of the Shades' scene from *La Bayadère*.

1964 29 February Antoinette Sibley dances Aurora in the Company's 400th performance of *The Sleeping Beauty*. **2 April** The Company's contributions to the celebrations of the 400th anniversary of Shakespeare's birth include Ashton's *The Dream*, which launches the dance partnership of Sibley and Anthony Dowell. **2 December** Bronislava Nijinska, younger sister of Nijinsky, revives her *Les Biches*, with Svetlana Beriosova as the Hostess.

1965 9 February MacMillan's first full-length work, *Romeo and Juliet*, is presented; created for Lynn Seymour and Christopher Gable, the opening night is danced by Fonteyn and Nureyev.

1966 23 March Nijinska revives her *Les Noces* in a double bill with *Les Biches*. **May** MacMillan takes up the ballet directorship of the Deutsche Oper Berlin. **19 May** MacMillan's *Song of the Earth*, created for Cranko's Stuttgart Ballet, is given its Covent Garden premiere.

1967 25 January Antony Tudor creates his first work for The Royal Ballet, *Shadowplay*.

1968 29 February The premiere of Nureyev's version of *The Nutcracker*. **26 April** The Company makes the official announcement of Ashton's retirement as Director in 1970 and his succession by MacMillan. **25 October** The premiere of Ashton's *Enigma Variations*. **12 November** Tudor revives his 1938 production of *Lilac Garden*.

1970s

1971 22 July MacMillan's long-awaited *Anastasia* opens, with Seymour in the lead role. **4 August** The premiere of American choreographer Glen Tetley's contemporary ballet *Field Figures*.

1972 20 June Natalia Makarova dances Giselle, partnered by Dowell, making her debut at Covent Garden as a Guest Artist.

1973 8 June At Covent Garden, Nureyev and Makarova dance *The Sleeping Beauty* together for the first time.

1974 7 March Sibley, Dowell and David Wall dance the opening night of MacMillan's *Manon*. **7 October** The premiere of MacMillan's *Elite Syncopations* with Wayne Sleep in the Principal Character role.

1975 April The Royal Ballet makes its first tour of the Far East.

1976 12 February The first performance of Ashton's *A Month in the Country*, with Dowell and Seymour.

1977 13 June Norman Morrice succeeds MacMillan as Director of The Royal Ballet.

1978 14 February The premiere of MacMillan's full-length ballet *Mayerling*, the Principal male role created for David Wall.

1980s

1980 13 March MacMillan's *Gloria* receives its premiere. **4 August** Ashton creates *Rhapsody* for Lesley Collier and Mikhail Baryshnikov, given at a performance for the 80th birthday of HM Queen Elizabeth The Queen Mother.

1981 30 April World premiere of MacMillan's *Isadora* with Merle Park in the title role, to celebrate the Company's golden jubilee.

1982 2 December The premiere of Nureyev's *The Tempest*.

1984 24 February MacMillan's *Different Drummer* is created for the Company. **20 December** Collier and Dowell perform in the first night of Peter Wright's Biedermeier-inspired production of *The Nutcracker*.

1986 Anthony Dowell is appointed Director of The Royal Ballet.

1987 12 March *Swan Lake*, with Cynthia Harvey and Jonathan Cope, is Dowell's first production as Director. **16 December** Ashton stages a revival of *Cinderella*, his final production for The Royal Ballet.

1988 9 March Bintley's *'Still Life' at the Penguin Café* receives its world premiere with the Company. **19 August** Ashton dies in the year in which his *Ondine* is revived by Dowell after an absence of 22 years from the repertory.

1989 18 May The full-length *La Bayadère* is given its premiere by The Royal Ballet in a new production by Makarova.
8 December MacMillan's final, full-evening production, *The Prince of the Pagodas*, is created for the Company, with Darcey Bussell and Jonathan Cope.

1990 19 July MacMillan's 'Farewell' *pas de deux* with Bussell and Irek Mukhamedov is performed at a London Palladium gala.

1991 7 February The first night of MacMillan's *Winter Dreams* (which grew out of the 'Farewell' *pas de deux*).
2 May In celebration of the 60th anniversary of the Company, Bintley's *Cyrano* is first performed at a Royal Gala.

1992 13 February William Forsythe's *In the middle, somewhat elevated* is first performed by the Company.
19 March MacMillan's last work, *The Judas Tree*, created for Mukhamedov and Viviana Durante, receives its premiere.
29 October MacMillan dies of a heart attack during the first performance of a major revival of his *Mayerling*.
6 December Ashton's *Tales of Beatrix Potter* is first staged by The Royal Ballet.

1993 7 April Baryshnikov's *Don Quixote* is first performed by the Company in new designs.

1994 6 April A new production of *The Sleeping Beauty* by Anthony Dowell is performed in Washington in the presence of the President of the USA and HRH The Princess Margaret. **18 June** Ashley Page's *Fearful Symmetries* is first performed (receiving the 1995 Olivier Award for Best New Dance Production). **3 November** Dowell's production of *The Sleeping Beauty* with designs by Maria Björnson is first performed at the Royal Opera House for a Royal Gala.

75

This page:

Mara Galeazzi and Paul Kay in Wayne McGregor's *Limen*

©ROH/Bill Cooper, 2009

2000s

1996 2 May MacMillan's *Anastasia* is performed with new sets and costumes by Bob Crowley.

1997 14 July Farewell Gala and final performance at the 'old' Royal Opera House. During the closure The Royal Ballet is 'on tour', performing at Labatt's Apollo, Hammersmith, the Royal Festival Hall and the Barbican.

1999 December The redeveloped Royal Opera House opens. The Royal Ballet's first programme is 'A Celebration of International Choreography'. **17 December** The opening night of *The Nutcracker* is the first performance of a full-length ballet in the new House.

2000 8 February Revival of De Valois' production of *Coppélia* in the original designs by Osbert Lancaster opens. **29 February** Ashton's *Marguerite and Armand* is revived with Sylvie Guillem and Nicolas Le Riche in the title roles. **6 May** Millicent Hodson and Kenneth Archer produce a major restaging of Nijinsky's *Jeux* in a programme with *L'Après-midi d'un faune*.

2001 8 March De Valois dies. **July** Dowell retires as Director of The Royal Ballet. **23 October** The first performance of Nureyev's version of *Don Quixote* by The Royal Ballet, which marks the first performance under Ross Stretton's tenure as Director. **22 November** The first performance by The Royal Ballet of Cranko's *Onegin*.

2002 9 February HRH The Princess Margaret, Countess of Snowdon, President of The Royal Ballet, dies. **September** Ross Stretton resigns as Director. **December** Monica Mason becomes Director of the Company.

2003 13 January The Company dances Jiří Kylián's *Sinfonietta* for the first time. **8 March** The premiere of Makarova's new production of *The Sleeping Beauty*. **22 December** Wendy Ellis Somes's new production of *Cinderella* receives its premiere.

2004 April The Royal Ballet pays homage to Sergey Diaghilev in a 75th-anniversary tribute programme that includes the Company premiere of *Le Spectre de la rose*. **4 November** The premiere of Ashton's full-length *Sylvia*, reconstructed and staged by Christopher Newton for the 'Ashton 100' celebrations.

2005 7 May The premiere of a new work by Christopher Bruce, inspired by the life of Jimi Hendrix: *Three Songs – Two Voices*.

76

2006 15 May The Company begins its 75th-anniversary celebrations with a new production of the 1946 *Sleeping Beauty*, realized by Monica Mason and Christopher Newton with Messel's original designs, re-created by Peter Farmer, followed by revivals of Ashton's *Homage to The Queen*, with additional new choreography by Christopher Wheeldon, Michael Corder and David Bintley, and De Valois' *The Rake's Progress*. **8 June** A gala performance of *Homage* preceded by *La Valse* and *divertissements* is attended by HM The Queen. **November** The premieres of Wayne McGregor's *Chroma* and Wheeldon's *DGV: Danse à grande vitesse*. **December** McGregor becomes Resident Choreographer of The Royal Ballet.

2007 March Alastair Marriott's *Children of Adam* receives its premiere. **April** Will Tuckett's *The Seven Deadly Sins* receives its premiere. **June** Barry Wordsworth is appointed Music Director. **8 June** Darcey Bussell retires as a Principal. **23 November** The Royal Ballet performs Balanchine's *Jewels* in its entirety for the first time.

2008 28 February The first performance of Wheeldon's *Electric Counterpoint*. **23 April** The mainstage choreographic debut of Kim Brandstrup with *Rushes: Fragments of a Lost Story*. **15 June-21 July** The Royal Ballet goes on tour in China and the Far East, performing in Beijing, Shanghai, Tokyo, Osaka and Hong Kong. **October** marks the 50th anniversary of Ashton's *Ondine*. **13 November** The premiere of McGregor's *Infra*. **28 December** The Royal Ballet's first live cinema broadcast – *The Nutcracker* with Alexandra Ansanelli and Valeri Hristov.

2009 March Anthony Russell Roberts retires as Artistic Administrator and is succeeded by Kevin O'Hare. **April** Jeanetta Laurence is appointed Associate Director of The Royal Ballet. **June–July** The Royal Ballet tours to Washington D.C., Granada and Havana. **4 November** Wayne McGregor's *Limen* receives its premiere in a mixed programme with Glen Tetley's *Sphinx*, which enters the repertory for the first time. **17 November** A service to dedicate a memorial to the founders of The Royal Ballet is held at Westminster Abbey.

2010 January 50th anniversary of Ashton's *La Fille mal gardée*. **19 February** Mainstage choreographic debut of Royal Ballet First Artist Jonathan Watkins with *As One*. **23 April** Miyako Yoshida dances her last performance with the Company at the Royal Opera House as Cinderella. **5 May** Mainstage choreographic debut of Royal Ballet First Artist Liam Scarlett with *Asphodel Meadows*. **June–July** The Royal Ballet tours to Japan for the tenth time (Tokyo and Osaka) and Spain (Barcelona). **29 June** Miyako Yoshida retires from the Company, dancing her last Juliet in Tokyo. **15 October** World Premiere of Brandstrup's *Invitus Invitam*.

2011 28 February World Premiere of Wheeldon's *Alice's Adventures in Wonderland*. **13 May** World Premiere of McGregor's *Live Fire Exercise*. **June–July** The Royal Ballet tours to Taiwan. **17-19 June** The Company appears at The O$_2$ Arena for the first time performing MacMillan's *Romeo and Juliet*.

2012 23 March The first ever 'Royal Ballet Live' is broadcast on the internet. **5 April** World Premiere of McGregor's *Carbon Life* and Scarlett's *Sweet Violets*. **2 June** MacMillan's *The Prince of the Pagodas* returns to the repertory after an absence of 16 years. **15–20 June** *Metamorphosis: Titian 2012*. **16 June** BP Big Screen. **20 June** After 54 years with the Company Monica Mason retires as Director, succeeded by Kevin O'Hare. **30 October** HM The Queen's diamond jubilee is celebrated in a gala performance. **2 November** Liam Scarlett is appointed The Royal Ballet's first Artist in Residence.

2013 22 February World Premieres of Ratmansky's *24 Preludes* and Wheeldon's *Aeternum*. **February/March** A group from The Royal Ballet travels to Brazil for gala performances and to attend a symposium on dance in education. **8 May** World Premiere of Scarlett's *Hansel and Gretel*. **24 May** World Premiere of McGregor's *Raven Girl*. **27 May** Pita's *The Metamorphosis* is broadcast on Sky Arts. **June** The Royal Ballet tours to Monte Carlo. **20 June** The world premiere of Kim Brandstrup's *Ceremony of Innocence* at the Aldeburgh Festival. **July** The Royal Ballet tours to Japan (Tokyo). Leanne Benjamin, Alina Cojocaru, Mara Galeazzi and Johan Kobborg leave the Company.

Alicia Markova

Alicia Markova was Britain's first prima ballerina, whose poise and artistry captured the imaginations of great choreographers and international audiences.

Born Lilian Alicia Marks on 1 December 1910 in London, her prodigious talent for dancing became apparent at a very young age and at just 14 she joined Sergey Diaghilev's Ballets Russes, with her name changed to the more Russian sounding Alicia Markova. Diaghilev, who Markova affectionately called 'Serjy-pop', predicted a great future for his 'dushka'. His sudden death in 1929 came as a terrible blow to the dancer. Her return to London at this time marked the start of an association with De Valois' Vic-Wells Ballet (later The Royal Ballet) and The Ballet Club (later Ballet Rambert), establishing Markova as the greatest ballerina of her generation, a unique influence on the evolution of British ballet and the two fledgling companies.

She danced many of the great classical solos and created new roles for choreographers including Antony Tudor, Ninette de Valois and Frederick Ashton. She was appointed Prima Ballerina of the Vic-Wells Ballet in 1933. On New Year's Day 1934 she became the first British ballerina to dance the title role in *Giselle* with Anton Dolin, her stage partner for over thirty years, as Albrecht. Audiences were enthralled by Markova's unique lightness and the purity of her line, and she soon became synonymous with the role.

Up to and during World War II she performed all over the world, receiving enormous critical acclaim

in America. Upon her return to Britain in 1950, she and Dolin established the Festival Ballet (later English National Ballet), which attracted some of the world's best dancers and toured extensively, playing a vital role in establishing ballet as an art form in Britain.

Markova was made a DBE in 1963 and in the same year announced her retirement from dancing. She assumed the role of Director of Ballet at the Metropolitan Opera, a role she held for six years, while at the same time lecturing and teaching. She never married, once saying that 'we in Britain never had a ballerina before me – and that was the whole point of my life'. Markova died on 2 December 1994, the day after her 94th birthday.

David Wall

In 1966, at the age of just 21, David Wall became the youngest male to be made Principal in the history of The Royal Ballet. A handsome redhead widely known as 'Ginger', Wall had a compelling stage presence and masculine allure that opened up new dramatic possibilities for the great choreographers of the day.

Wall's gift was recognized during ballroom dancing lessons at his primary school in Windsor. He joined The Royal Ballet School in 1956, aged 10, and upon graduation in 1963, the touring section of The Royal Ballet. The following year his partnership with Doreen Wells in Frederick Ashton's *Les Deux Pigeons* won them national acclaim and the pair quickly became the touring company's leading couple.

Following reorganization within The Royal Ballet in 1970, Wall moved to Covent Garden. He partnered leading ballerinas including Lynn Seymour and Margot Fonteyn, and Fonteyn later paid tribute to his artistic sensitivity, referring to him as her 'favourite'. He also had several roles created on him, most notably Crown Prince Rudolf in Kenneth MacMillan's 1978 ballet *Mayerling*. Wall's physical strength and dramatic intensity enabled him to realize the extremes of MacMillan's creation, and Crown Prince Rudolf is still regarded as the most emotionally demanding and physically challenging Principal male role in the repertory.

Wall retired from performing in 1984, joining the Royal Academy of Dance, where he spent seven years as Assistant Director and then Director. He was made

a CBE in 1985, and in 1995 became Ballet Master at English National Ballet. He and his wife, Alfreda Thorogood – who had herself been a Principal of The Royal Ballet – staged MacMillan's *The Sleeping Beauty* for ENB in 2005. Even after his retirement from ENB in 2007, Wall continued to share his extensive knowledge about MacMillan and his works.

Wall died on 18 June 2013. His stunning *jeté* is immortalized in the 1975 bronze statue by Enzo Plazzotta that can be seen on the Chelsea Embankment.

79

Principal Guest Artists and Principals

Carlos Acosta
Joined as Principal 1998
Principal Guest Artist 2003
Born: Havana, Cuba
Trained: National Ballet
School of Cuba
Previous Companies:
English National Ballet (1991),
National Ballet of Cuba (1992),
Houston Ballet (1993)

Federico Bonelli
Joined as Principal 2003
Born: Genoa, Italy
Trained: Turin Dance Academy
Previous Companies: Zurich
Ballet (1996), Dutch National
Ballet (1999)

Lauren Cuthbertson
Joined 2002
Promoted to Principal 2008
Born: Devon, England
Trained:
The Royal Ballet School

Nehemiah Kish
Joined as Principal 2010
Born: Michigan, USA
Trained: National Ballet
School of Canada
Previous Company: National
Ballet of Canada (2001),
Royal Danish Ballet (2008)

Sarah Lamb
Joined 2004
Promoted to Principal 2006
Born: Boston, USA
Trained: Boston Ballet School
Previous Company: Boston
Ballet (1998)

Roberta Marquez
Joined and promoted to
Principal 2004
Born: Rio de Janeiro, Brazil
Trained: Maria Olenewa State
Dance School
Previous Company:
Theatro Municipal, Rio de
Janeiro (1994)

Steven McRae
Joined 2004
Promoted to Principal 2009
Born: Sydney, Australia
Trained:
The Royal Ballet School

Laura Morera
Joined 1995
Promoted to Principal 2007
Born: Madrid, Spain
Trained:
The Royal Ballet School

Marianela Nuñez
Joined 1998
Promoted to Principal 2002
Born: Buenos Aires
Trained:
Teatro Colón Ballet School,
The Royal Ballet School

Natalia Osipova
Joined as Principal 2013
Born: Moscow
Trained: Bolshoi Ballet
Academy
Previous Company: Bolshoi
Ballet (2004), American Ballet
Theatre (2010), Mikhailovsky
Theatre (2011)

Rupert Pennefather
Joined 1999
Promoted to Principal 2008
Born: Maidenhead, England
Trained:
The Royal Ballet School

Thiago Soares
Joined 2002
Promoted to Principal 2006
Born: São Gonçalo, Brazil
Trained: Centre for Dance,
Rio de Janeiro
Previous Company:
Theatro Municipal, Rio de
Janeiro (1998)

Edward Watson
Joined 1994
Promoted to Principal 2005
Born: Bromley, England
Trained:
The Royal Ballet School

Zenaida Yanowsky
Joined 1994
Promoted to Principal 2001
Born: Lyon, France
Trained: Las Palmas, Majorca
Previous Company: Paris
Opéra Ballet (1994)

Principal Character Artists, Character Artists, First Soloists and Soloists

PRINCIPAL CHARACTER ARTISTS
Left to right:
Gary Avis
Alastair Marriott
Elizabeth McGorian
Genesia Rosato

Christopher Saunders

CHARACTER ARTIST
Philip Mosley

FIRST SOLOISTS
Left to right:
Alexander Campbell
Ricardo Cervera
Deirdre Chapman
Yuhui Choe

Helen Crawford
Bennet Gartside
Melissa Hamilton
Ryoichi Hirano

FIRST SOLOISTS
Left to right:
Valeri Hristov
Hikaru Kobayashi
Itziar Mendizabal
Johannes Stepanek

SOLOISTS
Left to right:
Christina Arestis
Claire Calvert
Olivia Cowley
Elizabeth Harrod

James Hay
Jonathan Howells
Fumi Kaneko
Paul Kay

Kenta Kura
Iohna Loots
Emma Maguire
Laura McCulloch

Kristen McNally
David Pickering
Beatriz Stix-Brunell
Akane Takada

83

Soloists, First Artists and Artists

SOLOISTS
Left to right:
Dawid Trzensimiech
Eric Underwood
Thomas Whitehead
Valentino Zucchetti

FIRST ARTISTS
Left to right:
Tara-Brigitte Bhavnani
Leanne Cope
Tristan Dyer
Hayley Forskitt

Meaghan Grace Hinkis
Nathalie Harrison
Francesca Hayward
Pietra Mello-Pittman

Fernando Montaño
Erico Montes
Sian Murphy
Yasmine Naghdi

Ludovic Ondiviela
Romany Pajdak
Michael Stojko
Lara Turk

Andrej Uspenski
Sabina Westcombe
James Wilkie

ARTISTS
Left to right:
Luca Acri
Ruth Bailey
Sander Blommaert
Camille Bracher

Annette Buvoli
Jacqueline Clark
Claudia Dean
David Donnelly

Artists

ARTISTS
Left to right:
Nicol Edmonds
Benjamin Ella
Kevin Emerton
Elsa Godard

Tierney Heap
Mayara Magri
Tomas Mock
Anna Rose O'Sullivan

Demelza Parish
Gemma Pitchley-Gale
Marcelino Sambé
Leticia Stock

Donald Thom

PRIX DE LAUSANNE DANCER
Masaya Yamamoto

Left to right:

Artistic Associate
Christopher Wheeldon

Associate Director
Jeanetta Laurence

Director
Kevin O'Hare

*Resident
Choreographer*
Wayne McGregor

Music Director
Barry Wordsworth

Photograph:
Elliott Franks

Artistic Staff
Back row left to right:
David Pickering,
Liam Scarlett,
Samantha Raine,
Jonathan Howells,
Philip Mosley,
Christopher Carr,
Christopher Saunders,
Gary Avis,
Jonathan Cope

Seated left to right:
Anna Trevien,
Lesley Collier,
Jeanetta Laurence,
Elizabeth Anderton,
Alexander Agadzhanov

Photograph:
Rob Moore

Administrative Staff
Standing left to right:
Kate Davis,
Hannah Mayhew,
Orsolo Ricciardeli,
Yvonne Hunte,
Andrew Hurst,
Susan Beavon,
Emma Southworth

Seated left to right:
Julia Lister,
Elizabeth Ferguson,
Alison Tedbury,
Poppy Ben David,
Heather Baxter

Photograph:
Rob Moore

Music Staff
Left to right:
Philip Cornfield,
Kate Shipway,
Nigel Bates,
Helen Nicholas,
Paul Stobart,
Robert Clark,
Barry Wordsworth,
Tim Qualtrough,
Jonathan Beavis

Photograph:
Rob Moore

**Royal Ballet
Healthcare Team**
Standing left to right:
Olivia Powell,
Frank Appel,
Jason Laird,
Britt-Tajet Foxell,
Jacqueline Birtwisle,
Jane Paris;

Seated left to right:
Konrad Simpson,
Moira McCormack,
Aedin Kennedy

Staff also includes:
Fiona Kleckham,
Helen Wellington,
Tatina Semprini,
Patrick Rump

Photograph:
Rob Moore

Stage Management
Left to right:
Lynne Otto,
Lucy Summers,
Johanna Adams Farley

Photograph:
Rob Moore

Artists and Staff

The Royal Ballet 2013/14

Patron HM The Queen
President HRH The Prince of Wales
Vice-President The Lady Sarah Chatto

Director Kevin O'Hare
Associate Director Jeanetta Laurence

Music Director Barry Wordsworth
Resident Choreographer
Wayne McGregor CBE

Artistic Associate Christopher Wheeldon

General Manager
Heather Baxter

*Company Manager
and Tour Manager*
Andrew Hurst

*Artistic Administrator
and Character Artist*
Philip Mosley

Contracts Administrator
Alison Tedbury

*Deputy Company
Manager*
Elizabeth Ferguson

*Assistant to the
Directors and Artistic
Co-ordinator*
Julia Lister

*Administrative
Co-ordinator*
Yvonne Hunte

Financial Controller
Susan Beavon

*Management
Accountant*
Orsola Ricciardelli

**Clinical Director,
Ballet Healthcare**
Gregory Retter

*Head of
Physiotherapy
and Chartered
Physiotherapist*
Moira McCormack

*Chartered
Physiotherapists*
Aedin Kennedy
Jason Laird

*Body Control
Instructors*
Jane Paris
Fiona Kleckham

*Occupational
Psychologist*
Britt Tajet-Foxell

Masseurs
Tatina Semprini
Konrad Simpson
Helen Wellington

Sports Scientists
Patrick Rump
Frank Appel

*Consultant
Orthopaedic
Surgeon*
Lloyd Williams

Medical Advisor
Ian Beasley

*Healthcare Team
Assistant*
Olivia Powell

Ballet Masters
Christopher Saunders
Gary Avis

Ballet Mistress
Samantha Raine

*Assistant Ballet
Master*
Jonathan Howells

*Senior Teacher and
Répétiteur to the
Principal Artists*
Alexander
Agadzhanov

Répétiteurs
Lesley Collier
Jonathan Cope

Dance Notator
Anna Trevien

*Education Administrator
and Teacher*
David Pickering

Artist in Residence
Liam Scarlett

Head of Music Staff
Robert Clark

Music Staff
Jonathan Beavis
Richard Coates
Philip Cornfield
Tim Qualtrough
Kate Shipway
Paul Stobart

Music Administrator
Nigel Bates

*Jette Parker Young
Artist Pianist*
Helen Nicholas

**Studio Programme
Senior Producer**
Emma Southworth

Producer
Poppy Ben David

*Administrative
Co-ordinator*
Hannah Mayhew

**Guest Principal
Ballet Master**
Christopher Carr

Principal Guest Teacher
Elizabeth Anderton

Guest Teachers
Boris Akimov
Jacquelin Barrett
Johnny Eliasen
Olga Evreinoff
Antonia Franceschi
Desmond Kelly
Roland Price

Conductors
David Briskin
Boris Gruzin
Valeriy Ovsyanikov
Tom Seligman
Pavel Sorokin
Martin West
Barry Wordsworth
Martin Yates

Principals
Carlos Acosta†
Federico Bonelli
Lauren Cuthbertson
Matthew Golding††
Nehemiah Kish
Sarah Lamb
Roberta Marquez
Steven McRae
Laura Morera
Marianela Nuñez
Natalia Osipova
Rupert Pennefather
Thiago Soares
Cory Stearns††
Edward Watson
Zenaida Yanowsky

**Principal
Character
Artists**
Gary Avis
Alastair Marriott
Elizabeth McGorian
Genesia Rosato
Christopher Saunders
William Tuckett††

First Soloists
Alexander Campbell
Ricardo Cervera
Deirdre Chapman
Yuhui Choe
Helen Crawford
Bennet Gartside
Melissa Hamilton
Ryoichi Hirano
Valeri Hristov
Hikaru Kobayashi
Itziar Mendizabal
Johannes Stepanek

Soloists
Christina Arestis
Claire Calvert
Olivia Cowley
Elizabeth Harrod
James Hay
Jonathan Howells
Fumi Kaneko
Paul Kay
Kenta Kura
Iohna Loots
Emma Maguire
Laura McCulloch
Kristen McNally
David Pickering
Beatriz Stix-Brunell
Akane Takada
Dawid Trzensimiech
Eric Underwood
Thomas Whitehead
Valentino Zucchetti

First Artists
Tara-Brigitte Bhavnani
Leanne Cope
Tristan Dyer
Hayley Forskitt
Francesca Hayward
Meaghan Grace Hinkis
Nathalie Harrison
Pietra Mello-Pittman
Fernando Montaño
Erico Montes
Sian Murphy
Yasmine Naghdi
Ludovic Ondiviela
Romany Pajdak
Michael Stojko
Lara Turk
Andrej Uspenski
Sabina Westcombe
James Wilkie

Artists
Luca Acri
Ruth Bailey
Sander Blommaert
Camille Bracher
Annette Buvoli
Jacqueline Clark
Claudia Dean
David Donnelly
Nicol Edmonds
Benjamin Ella
Kevin Emerton
Elsa Godard
Tierney Heap
Mayara Magri
Tomas Mock
Anna Rose O'Sullivan
Demelza Parish
Gemma Pitchley-Gale
Marcelino Sambé
Leticia Stock
Donald Thom

Prix de Lausanne dancer
Masaya Yamamoto

† **Principal Guest Artist**
††**Guest Artist**

**Governors of the
Royal Ballet Companies**

Chairman
Dame Jenny
   Abramsky DBE

Professor Michael
   Clarke CBE DL
Ricki Gail Conway
The Marchioness
   of Douro OBE
Dame Vivien
   Duffield DBE

Stephen Hough
Desmond Kelly OBE
Thomas Lynch
Gail Monahan
Christopher Nourse
Marguerite Porter
Simon Robey

Dame Sue Street DCB
Monica Zamora

Honorary Secretary
Peter Wilson

In 1956 Queen Elizabeth II granted the then Sadler's Wells Ballet, Sadler's Wells Theatre Ballet and Sadler's Wells School a Royal Charter, and they became respectively The Royal Ballet and Royal Ballet School. Under the Charter a body of Governors was set up whose ultimate duty it is to safeguard the future of the Company (now The Royal Ballet and Birmingham Royal Ballet) and School and to be the custodians of the traditions established by Dame Ninette de Valois in the formation of the Company and School in 1931.

The Royal Ballet on DVD and Blu-ray

WWW.ROH.ORG.UK/SHOP

Romeo and Juliet
The Royal Ballet
Music: Prokofiev
Choreography: MacMillan
Cast: Cuthbertson, Bonelli,
Campbell, Gartside, Saunders,
Artists of The Royal Ballet.
Orchestra of the Royal Opera
House/Wordsworth
Recorded 2012
Opus Arte DVD/Blu-ray

Ashton Celebration
The Royal Ballet
Music: Ravel, Massenet,
Johan Strauss II, Satie, Liszt
Choreography: Ashton
Cast: Benjamin, Hristov, Choe,
Campbell, Kish, Watson, Nuñez,
Maguire, Takada, Trzensimiech,
Rojo, Polunin, Saunders, Avis,
Artists of The Royal Ballet.
Orchestra of the Royal Opera
House/Plasson
Recorded 2013
Opus Arte DVD/Blu-ray

Tchaikovsky Collection
The Royal Ballet
Music: Tchaikovsky
Choreography: Petipa, Ivanov;
Petipa; Wright after Ivanov
Cast: Nuñez, Soares, Saunders;
Cojocaru, Bonelli, Nuñez,
Rosato; Yoshida, McRae, Avis,
Loots, Cervera.
Orchestra of the Royal Opera
House/Ovsyanikov/Kessels
Recorded 2006/09
Opus Arte DVD/Blu-ray

**An Evening With
The Royal Ballet**
Music: Adam, Délibes, Hérold,
Prokofiev, Stravinsky, Tchaikovsky
Choreography: Ashton, De Valois,
Dowell, Fokine, Ivanov, MacMillan,
Nijinska, Petipa, Wheeldon, Wright
Cast: Artists of The Royal Ballet.
Orchestra of the Royal Opera
House/Bond, Carewe,
Gruzin, Kessels, Moldoveanu,
Ovsyanikov, Twiner, Royal Ballet
Sinfonia/Gruzin
Recorded 2000–11
Opus Arte DVD/Blu-ray

**Frederick Ashton:
Les Patineurs •
Divertissements
• Scènes de ballet**
The Royal Ballet
Music: Meyerbeer (*Les Patineurs*),
Various (*Divertissements*),
Stravinsky (*Scènes de ballet*)
Choreography: Ashton
Cast: McRae, Bussell, Cope, Rojo,
Benjamin, Acosta, Yoshida, Putrov,
Artists of The Royal Ballet.
Royal Ballet Sinfonia/Murphy
Orchestra of the Royal Opera
House/Wordsworth.
Recorded 2004/10
Opus Arte DVD

**Three Ballets
by Kenneth MacMillan**
The Royal Ballet
Music: Joplin (*Elite Syncopations*),
Elias (*The Judas Tree*),
Shostakovich (*Concerto*)
Choreography: MacMillan
Casts: Lamb, Galeazzi, Hristov,
McRae/Acosta, Benjamin, Watson,
Gartside/Choe, McRae, Nuñez,
Pennefather, Crawford.
Orchestra of the Royal Opera
House/Clark, Wordsworth, Grier.
Recorded 2010
Opus Arte DVD/Blu-ray

**Three Ballets
by Wayne McGregor**
The Royal Ballet
Music: Talbot, Jack White III
(*Chroma*), Richter (*Infra*),
Saariaho (*Limen*)
Choreography: McGregor
Casts: Benjamin, Bonelli,
Cuthbertson, Galeazzi, Hamilton,
Lamb, McRae, Nuñez, Rojo,
Underwood, Watson.
Orchestra of the Royal Opera
House/Capps, Wordsworth
The Max Richter Quintet
Recorded 2006/8/9
Opus Arte DVD/Blu-ray

**Alice's Adventures in
Wonderland**
The Royal Ballet
Music: Talbot
Choreography: Wheeldon
Cast: Cuthbertson, Polunin, Watson,
Yanowsky, Saunders, McRae, Beale,
Artists of The Royal Ballet.
Orchestra of the Royal Opera
House/Wordsworth
Recorded 2011
Opus Arte DVD/Blu-ray

La Bayadère
The Royal Ballet
Music: Minkus
Choreography: Makarova/Petipa
Cast: Rojo, Acosta, Nuñez,
Artists of The Royal Ballet.
Orchestra of the Royal Opera
House/Ovsyanikov
Recorded 2009
Opus Arte DVD/Blu-ray

Ondine
The Royal Ballet
Music: Henze
Choreography: Ashton
Cast: Yoshida, Watson,
Rosato, Cervera, Avis,
Artists of The Royal Ballet.
Orchestra of the Royal Opera
House/Wordsworth
Recorded 2010
Opus Arte DVD/Blu-ray

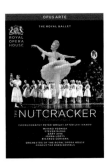

The Nutcracker
The Royal Ballet
Music: Tchaikovsky
Choreography: Wright/Ivanov
Cast: Yoshida, McRae, Avis,
Loots, Cervera.
Orchestra of the Royal Opera
House/Kessels
Recorded 2010
Opus Arte DVD/Blu-ray

Swan Lake
The Royal Ballet
Music: Tchaikovsky
Choreography: Petipa/Ivanov
Cast: Nuñez, Soares, McGorian,
Saunders, Marriott, Pickering,
Artists of The Royal Ballet.
Orchestra of the Royal Opera
House/Ovsyanikov
Recorded 2009
Opus Arte DVD/Blu-ray

Mayerling
The Royal Ballet
Music: Liszt (arr. Lanchbery)
Choreography: MacMillan
Cast: Watson, Galeazzi, Lamb,
Artists of The Royal Ballet.
Orchestra of the Royal Opera
House/Wordsworth
Recorded 2009
Opus Arte DVD/Blu-ray

Dido and Aeneas
The Royal Opera/The Royal Ballet
Music: Purcell
Choreography: McGregor
Cast: Connolly, Meacham, Crowe,
Fulgoni, Artists of The Royal Ballet.
Orchestra of the Age of
Enlightenment/Hogwood
Recorded 2009
Opus Arte DVD/Blu-ray

Acis and Galatea
The Royal Opera/The Royal Ballet
Music: Handel
Choreography: McGregor
Cast: De Niese, Cuthbertson,
Workman, Watson, Agnew, McRae,
Rose, Underwood, Park, Kay,
Artists of The Royal Ballet.
Orchestra of the Age of
Enlightenment/Hogwood
Royal Opera Extra Chorus
Recorded 2009
Opus Arte DVD/Blu-ray

Manon
The Royal Ballet
Music: Massenet
Choreography: MacMillan
Cast: Rojo, Acosta, Martín,
Saunders, Morera, Artists of
The Royal Ballet.
Orchestra of the Royal Opera
House/Yates
Recorded 2008
DECCA DVD

Books

Dancers: Behind the Scenes with The Royal Ballet

By Andrej Uspenski

A collection of exclusive photographs, taken by Royal Ballet dancer Andrej Uspenski. Includes backstage photographs, as well as a number of breathtaking images taken from the wings. A unique photographic record, perfect for all ballet fans. Oberon Books, 2013

ISBN 978-1-84943-388-4

Titian Metamorphosis

A visually stunning celebration of the unique collaboration between the National Gallery and The Royal Ballet: *Metamorphosis: Titian 2012*. Art / Books in association with The Royal Opera House, 2013

ISBN 978-1-90897-004-6

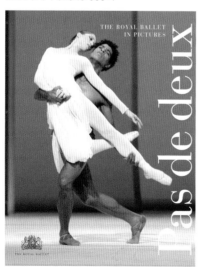

Pas de deux: The Royal Ballet in Pictures

More than two hundred stunning colour and black and white photographs of The Royal Ballet in rehearsal and performance. Oberon Books, 2007

ISBN 978-1-84002-777-8

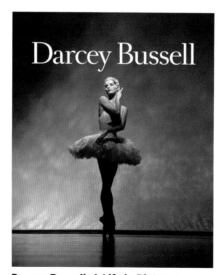

Darcey Bussell: A Life in Pictures

With photographs from Lord Snowdon, Mario Testino, Annie Liebovitz, Bill Cooper, Johan Persson and many more, *Darcey Bussell: A Life in Pictures* is a beautiful photographic celebration of one of the greatest English ballerinas of all time. Hardie Grant Books, 2012

ISBN 978-1-74270-352-7

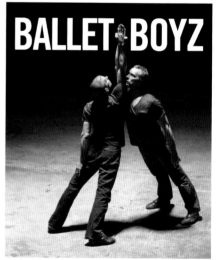

Ballet Boyz

Michael Nunn and WIlliam Trevitt were leading dancers with The Royal Ballet. This book celebrates ten years of their company, Ballet Boyz. Oberon Books, 2011

ISBN 978-1-84943-050-0

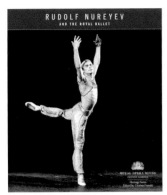

Rudolf Nureyev and The Royal Ballet

Black and white photographs documenting Rudolf Nureyev's long association with The Royal Ballet, edited by Cristina Franchi. Oberon Books, 2005

ISBN 978-1-84002-462-3

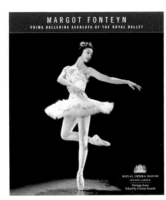

Margot Fonteyn: Prima Ballerina Assoluta of The Royal Ballet

Black and white photographs documenting Margot Fonteyn's long association with The Royal Ballet, edited by Cristina Franchi. Oberon Books, 2004

ISBN 978-1-84002-460-9

Frederick Ashton: Founder Choreographer of The Royal Ballet

Black and white photographs documenting Frederick Ashton's career and works made for The Royal Ballet, edited by Cristina Franchi. Oberon Books, 2004

ISBN 978-1-84002-461-6

Royal Opera House Souvenir Guide

By The Royal Opera House

Explore the Royal Opera House, its history, performance, architecture and backstage. Oberon Books, 2012

ISBN 978-1-84943-167-5

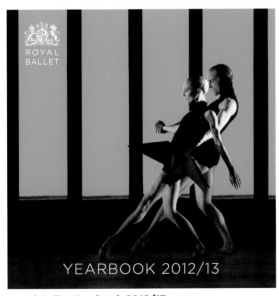

Royal Ballet Yearbook 2012/13

A summary of the ballets and exhibitions from last year also contains special interview features about dance partnerships and filming the Company on stage for cinema. Oberon Books, 2012

ISBN 978-1-84943-207-8

The Royal Ballet: 75 years

By Zoë Anderson

A history of The Royal Ballet since its inception to the present day. Faber & Faber, 2006

ISBN 978-0-57122-795-2

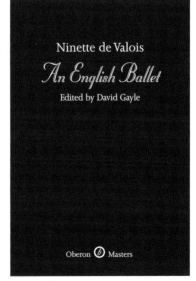

An English Ballet

By Ninette de Valois
Edited by David Gayle

Historic talk and essay from the Founder of The Royal Ballet. Oberon Books, 2011

ISBN 978-1-84943-107-1